INNER JOURNEY TO SACRED PLACES

INNER
JOURNEY
—TO—
SACRED
PLACES

DAVID ROOMY

PENTLAND PRESS, INC.
ENGLAND•USA•SCOTLAND

PUBLISHED BY PENTLAND PRESS, INC.
5124 Bur Oak Circle, Raleigh, North Carolina 27612
United States of America
919-782-0281

ISBN 1-57197-035-5
Library of Congress Catalog Card Number 96-69359

Printed in the United States of America

Contents

Acknowledgment

The author gratefully acknowledges the Process Work Education Society of Vancouver, British Columbia for helping fund the publishing of this book.

Introduction

Where the creative edge in psychology links the sacred inner world with healing, we shall journey. To the frontiers of the body and of life's big questions, illnesses and relationships, we shall go, applying a new methodology.

In one of my dreams I pass a thirteenth century hospital and enter an adjacent chapel lit with candles and merging into a prehistoric cave. In awe of this place, I am aware of its representing the connection between the sacred inner world and healing. Such has been my experience in a lifetime of therapeutic work with people and with myself.

Jungian and process psychology—which have grown from common roots—are particularly gifted in opening the door to the transpersonal which is at the same time transformative (chapter two). Both ground themselves in experience (empiricism) and sensory data, a natural protection when dealing with the intangibles of inner life. We shall see them up against such symptoms as the intransigent pain of a nun, following upon her three surgeries for cancer.

The book itself will unfold in this way. Always the experiences of modern people doing process work will be aligned with the deeper background in myth, alchemy, and Western and Eastern religions. Dream work and the inner journey will be counterpoised with background on healing practices in the ancient world. Subjective experiences of people will be balanced by objective data drawn from history, archeology, and mythology. This comparative approach suffuses all our material.

Many people carry wounds to the inner spirit or person. Other more obvious wounds may not heal. The key seems to lie in first touching where the spirit or inner person has been injured.

Surprisingly, this may happen through contacting information which lies in the body and which is dreamlike in nature.

Deciphering the information which lies in unfamiliar territory of the human being is the special forte of the two psychologies I have chosen to use. Our journey will take us into more complete understanding of these fields. And we shall start with the kinds of journeys people take in their night dreams. We shall pay particular attention to the dreams which take the dreamer to places which have about them a feeling of awe, mystery and fascination (chapter one). These dreams, opening one to a larger reality, may give healing to the wounded self. Actually these wounds to our deeper psyche may be trying to heal themselves, not only in our dreams but in our relationship difficulties and even our body symptoms.

We shall follow that process in the body, in perceptual systems, movement, feeling, spontaneous visualization and active inner dialog. We shall learn about ways of working with these processes which express an understanding of what is trying to happen beyond a person's present identity. In chapter three we shall compare process and Jungian inner work to Eastern and Western disciplines of meditation, and show the genius of these new psychological fields.

Continuing with our motif, we shall look at ancient places which appear in our dreams and which have a mystery to them. We may discover about those who painted Greek urns, for example, that the basic patterns which motivate life for people today, were present in them, our ancient kin. Jung has called these patterns the archetypes.

We shall be paying special attention to an archetype which is represented by the image of the old city, sometimes within four walls. This same image also represents itself as the square enclosed garden, with a fountain in the center, and it is the ship laden with every good thing (chapter five). This is the archetype of the self. In other eras and in non-psychological terminology, it is divine-like; it seems to regulate the life journey, continuing ever to bring it to realization and wholeness.

In years past people have often circled such a sacred place as an old city's center or garden's fountain or house of a sacred object. This centering process is universal. But again what is sacred in the center must be made known. And for this we have the resource of the inner life and the discipline of inner work. We have also the guidance of the methodologies we are using.

The inquiry we shall undergo in chapter three around "centering" has a deep link, through alchemy, to our investigation of the symbology of the self and the ancient city; it also is deeply connected to the creation of "the diamond body," our subjects in a cluster of chapters.

As we go deeper in our search we touch upon realities which in other ages have been the sole province of religion and philosophy. We ask ourselves such basic questions as: What is the myth or meaning behind my individual life? Does something go beyond this lifetime? And what is contemplation?

Following the processes of these questions themselves is deeply connected to healing our symptoms and relationships. Again, depth psychology may be of assistance as we unravel, with the help of Jung's understanding of alchemy for example, the symbol of the old city, and more of the meaning of our own sacred space. With the discussion of the diamond body we go to the frontiers of death itself and pose a possible answer . . . and more questions through exercises.

Any psychology which is worth its weight in gold touches on these basic questions of life. For an individual to come up with real answers which are grounded in experience may be possible. Some of the basic questions which have arisen out of the work of people I know concern: 1) the personal myth, 2) the frontier after death, and 3) the transpersonal.

The modern person clearly needs a myth by which to live. That myth can be a collective one or a personal one, or a combination of both; hence, our search in the depths of the psyche for what elicits awe and appreciation.

One concept or question worthy of our contemplation is what may be beyond this life. Jung felt that this is a question to which every person must try to formulate an answer, even if that person should fail. Jung also said that the crucial question of a person's life is whether that person is related to something transpersonal or not.

All these questions are interlinked. Myth links one to something beyond one's ego. Myths, either collective or personal, often are an attempt to answer vital questions such as why have we come into this life and whether something may go beyond it. Myth, the idea of something beyond this life, the transpersonal—all these belong together. They feature strongly in the processes that happen to modern people, or secondary processes.

We shall consider the intuitions which arise in depth psychology about connections to other times of history and their meanings for our own personal myths (chapter eight). We shall unfold a story from that point which involves relationship healing among people who happen to be of different religious persuasions and ethnic groups. Always we shall have our ear to the ground for developments in the individual psyche which have potential meaning for rapprochement in the larger social spheres. Finally, I shall have the joy of sharing my excitement with the discovery of the parallel between my dream of the inner chapel and the Grail. This I hope will throw light upon your reading of dreams and upon some of the great questions of our times, to which, I believe, the Grail speaks in the dreams of modern people. Following your dreams over the years with appropriate guidance, I shall show, can be like a Grail experience.

Here we pause for a further note of introduction about our guides: Jungian psychology is a comparative method par excellence. Jungian work finds parallels between the dream life of modern individuals and the classic "stuff" of human culture. These historical parallels drawn from diverse cultures become our reference points as we delve into the meaning of individual symbols on our journey to sacred places. Process work is the field developed by the analyst Arnold Mindell. It grew from roots in Jungian psychology. It takes seriously the dream, symptom, and relationship problem, being aware of what is trying to happen in these conditions. Process is like the wave equation of Heisenberg, "a tendency for something," and the "becoming" of philosophy. This inner process is spontaneous and has the fluidity of mercury.

All our chapters will have theoretical formulations which tie various aspects of the transpersonal with the new, process work and with Jungian psychology. In all of them as well, will be experiences of modern people, a touch of poetry, and/or exercises for the reader to do on her, or his own exploring of these frontiers.

Our motif of the sacred inner place can ultimately lead to where wounds are healed, and where they give way to wider spiritual and psychological unfoldment. But I am interested in your experience. What light may Jungian and process psychology throw upon all these questions? Here the fields which deal with the transpersonal are joined by psychology. What is it that such psychology can offer a modern person? That I hope you will discover in your own personal way as you interact with the material into which we now plunge.

one

Inner Journey
to Sacred Places

I am in awe of certain inner places. I am aware of their representing the connection between the sacred inner world and healing. In my experience, they are places I visit and revisit in my dreams and inner world.

I wonder if you the reader have had a dream of such a place, perhaps featuring an old city, which is both familiar and at the same time partly unfamiliar? Perhaps old cities have simply held a fascination for you.

Where process and Jungian work takes place is also a sacred place for me. I wish to convey a sense of healing in examples throughout the book.

The sacred, various writers tell us, is associated with qualities of fascination and MYSTERIUM TREMENDUM. One Greek word for the sacred, "heiros," means "superior, distinguished, not coercible, strong."[1]

The function of the sacred is to guide one to what is really important in one's life. A feeling of awe about one's dreams is the psyche's way of saying to you: your underlying reality, in the stuff of the inner life and meaning, is what you are about. It can clarify one's outer life of decision and action. The sacred inner spaces can be healing.

The inner landscape of sacred places can be worked with in a process way. A dream of mine said I was too tired to do the inner work on this dream but that a young anima figure[2] (unknown to me in outer life) could act out this process for me. It is important for me to be personal here at the beginning. I must do my own inner world around this theme. And you may see as the chapter

progresses, that such inner work appeared to be strongly connected to the processes of others as things turned out.

*A sample of inner process work; using active imagination
with a dream figure*

In the dream I was in the sacred spot of the acropolis in
Athens, not exactly like the one I know from outer life. The dream
emphasized an orientation to three mountains in three directions,
with the vacant sea in the fourth direction. At least one of the
mountains was so high it was white and snowy on the summit.
Snow balanced the hot climate below, just as three mountains in
their reaching for the heights of spirit were balanced by the sea—
the depths of the unconscious psyche. In this setting I was in the
center, at the center point of the greatness—greatness not of my
own but of nature. The Being of the mountains was part of this,
and they were not just any mountains, they were Hymettos,
Lykabettos, and the acropolis, and all with very powerful meanings
to me. I'll come back to the objective material associated to these
mountains in the next section.

The important fourth, completing the other three, was the sea,
the hidden world giving life to all forms. The unity of opposites
was suggested in all these forms. This was like a mandala set out
upon the earth, a circle, of landscape in this case, divided by four
points, and including the heights and depths as well. This dream
helped me prepare for a workshop. It also helped me with the specific theme of "Inner Journeys to Sacred Places," the theme of
that workshop and of this book. With a minor loss in my world at
that time, my emotion seemed to be compensated by the dream's
pointing to my next task. Not only that, the dream seemed to
enrich my understanding of how to approach that task.

I believed always before I had been stuck somehow with a feeling that I must travel to the sacred places in outer reality. Now
through this dream, the possibility presented itself to open up the
vistas of the sacred spaces with the help of inner dream figures, in
my case the anima. The latter would point to a new approach to
this material in the workshop. The peregrination, or sacred pil-

grimage, was an inner journey to be elucidated by the work of the inner guide, the anima.

The sacred space is to visit or circumambulate the center. The center is the place of greatness of the self, the guiding factor toward wholeness or fulfillment.

The animated psyche or soul knows what it is to be in a sacred space. The dream indicated I should turn over the inner work around this dream experience to the anima, or soul. What does it mean to meet our inner experience with the help of the soul or inner person? That inner quality of ourselves, soul, is more reflective and more receptive to the hidden reaches of the inner world. I need the guidance of this anima to search out these depths.

Sometimes this inner quality or anima wants to look around. In some people, she is the quality that likes to go to places which have history. These historical sites have a place in my inner world.

I want you the reader to be able to work with this soul quality as you touch the places that are important, even sacred in your memory, imagination and inner world. I want you to be able to make the journey there. And with the mediation of this soul-quality in yourselves, perhaps you can even process what comes up. I'll be giving you an example of how that worked for me, next. And at the end of the chapter there will be exercises for you.

I wanted to see if the anima, the young woman in my dream, would help me act out this dream experience, in active imagination. The anima, the soul, saw these mountain cones with different eyes than I, as a man do. She said at the end of the meditation: "These are my body. These sustain me." These words were a complete surprise to me, as they felt as if they had come from some other source in myself than the ego.

The anima figure was referring to the experience of the mountains. She took her hand up the rising line of the acropolis. Then she saw Lykabettos as a breast. She saw Hymettos as a mighty roll of a woman, the earth represented in a statue of herself. The horns of Salamis she felt as her own two breasts. The sea, by contrast, she waved her hands by, and thought to herself to leave it to me (to work on). Then she was in the earth mother Gaia's own center where the axes of lines connecting the various mountains crossed each other on the acropolis, and it was here she exclaimed, "These are my body. These sustain me."

I felt alive, fresh. I was glad to have become acquainted with how the anima experienced this landscape. Then she left this experience in my body. My body is really quite different than the way I have been looking upon it. I experience myself as somehow a part of the earth and these dramatic peaks, together with the sea. In my own body I partake of the landscape of the great mother, and of the self. This sustains me.

In this book we shall be using Jungian and process work as methodologies for getting to know more completely our inner places.

How process work, works

In the chapter, "Centering: The Journey into the Mandala," I shall be talking about the basics of process work in a way that people can use to work on their own.[3] In the process perspective, our experience is available to us in various channels of information such as visual, auditory, proprioception or feeling in the body, movement or kinesthesis, relationship and the world of synchronicities. Many times the channels of information may be shifting from one to another. But it is possible that we are not always aware of this process. It has long been a perspective of active imagination—the Jungian form of inner work—that different people were able to do this in different channels of information. For example, persons of certain natures painted their dreams while others of a different disposition danced theirs. The genius which Mindell expressed in his process work was to observe that shifts were taking place among these channels of information all the time the clients were working or in various ways presenting their material. Inner work and work with clients becomes a matter of following this process as it shifts among the various channels of information. This puts a new and additional cast upon the concept of following another person's or one's own process. It also involves awareness of primary and secondary process, to which we shall return later.[4]

In the piece of my own inner world, which I just described, you can see this shifting among the channels of information being followed. First I see through the animal's eyes (visual). Then the hand, as I experience it in my body (proprioception), starts to move (kinesthesis). She took her hand up the rising line she perceived as the acropolis' mounting of rock into the air. Then she saw (visual) Hymettos. Next as she gazed at Salamis, she felt the horns of the earth mother's breasts as her own body (proprioception). Finally, as she became aware of the crossing of the axes of these points on the top surface of the acropolis, at the shrine of Gaia, she exclaimed (auditory) in surprising words: "These (mountains) are my body. They sustain me."

My primary process (that with which I was identified) at the time of the dream was disappointing emotion and fatigue. My secondary process was to be opened to a big, internal process in which I could draw upon the resources of the greater psyche. This also brought information to me on inner work and creativity. The secondary process often is opposite to that with which I am identified. It happens to one in a dream, relationship problem or physical symptom. And often it points to the bigger meaning of one's life. Healing throughout ancient Greece was characteristically associated with the unification of opposites, in our language, the primary and secondary processes. We shall be returning to the topic of inner work, from a process methodology, at various times throughout our discussions. For those who may want to use this method, specific exercises will be provided.

A dream amplified by history, archeology and mythology

Now that we have experienced more what the intuitive quality of anima could tell us about this sacred spot, the acropolis in Athens, it is time to turn to the more objective side of things. We shall look at the site of the acropolis from what history and archeology, coupled with mythology, can tell us. As sites go, this outcropping of high rock in the midst of a great plain creates a perfect citadel; this, with its other features, makes the acropolis one of the most outstanding natural sites in the world. Moreover, each of these other features are not just beautiful in their own right, but they form part of the whole site of the acropolis; they belong to that site and that site to them. And, each of these other mountains has a special feeling and mythological character which they contribute in addition to their beauty, and balance of position, to the acropolis.

The acropolis itself possesses such mythological and imaginative material. But we shall first look to the three mountains which lie around it. Hymettos is known as the sleeping woman. Like the acropolis, it has always been regarded as a sacred mountain. This isn't surprising; when the earth throws up a figure of a great woman, stretching across one whole side of horizon, it is as if nature has cast up an image of herself for the human being to see. The cones or the horns of the great mother's figure in the landscape were always the most important reference point in ancient Greek architecture. At the site sacred to Asklepios, god of healing, at Epidauros, it was the earth that was regarded as the source of healing.[5]

Lykabettos is a perfect cone and of great size. Today on her crown is one of those small Greek white chapels. The cone suggests the breast. Lykabettos has always been associated with Aphrodite, goddess of love, without whose presence there is no healing.[6]

To the west of the acropolis and opposite the horns of Hymettos lie the horns of Salamis. They comprise, as horns, another sacred feature of Greek landscape in addition to the cone. Both the cone and the horns were the features of the land to which the early Greeks, especially those of the harmonious Minoan times, attributed the greatest significance. Both formations suggested to the early religious attitude, the powerful, life-sustaining substance of the Great Mother as earth or Gaia. She was body, and in her our bodies live—and live today. The Salamis horns also reminded Greeks of the favor accorded them in the naval defeat of the Persians in the Gulf of Salamis—an event favorably forecast by the oracle of Delphi—allowing for Athens' cultural ascendancy.

Three mountains with the sea on the fourth of the compass points suggest the presence of Artemis.[7] Artemis is the protector of wild animals and things wild. In my dream, the sheer quality of mountains on three sides with the sea in the position of the fourth suggested to me awe and the wild, uncompromising quality of nature. Carol Barnes Lucerno writes of Artemis: "She seems to stand for spiritual freedom and also distancing." Lucerno then goes on to quote from Walter Otto's *The Homeric Gods* in which he writes further of Artemis: "Nature is the mirror of divine femininity . . . a free nature with its brilliance and wildness, with its guiltless purity and uncanniness, the tender solitude of the maiden . . . "[8] (This also suggests the young anima figure who both helps me interpret the scene and is that scene; she also enables me to react to the dream and my life in spiritual freedom.)

Now we are ready to examine another dimension of the acropolis. This is the part which fascinates me most. The summit of the acropolis lies on the axis between Hymettos and the horns of Salamis. Further, a cross axis is created by the intersection of two powerful lines: one, the line running between the two stone maidens, or caryatids of the Erechtheion and the seventh column of the north facade of the Parthenon, and two, the line between Lykabettos on the northeast and the northwest corner of the Parthenon. Where those two axes intersect was the plaque to Gaia, or Ge. Thus she unites all the buildings as well as the natural forms of the important mountains. In her, all these qualities are unified. [9]

Artistically and historically this has tremendous interest to me. It means great though the Parthenon was, it really has its place among other sculpted forms and ancient sacred mountains which center in the earth mother. Human cultural achievement, however great, is related to a still greater natural center in the psyche, and this center implies all historical and cultural continuity (the collective unconscious).

In my experience there often seemed a call to go to Greece. Also, often I wished to visit Norwich in Norfolk. This English homeland had often appeared in my dreams as a sacred place, in the years after my return from England to the continent of North America. For Greece, it was often the town of Nafplion, which appeared in my dreams. Nafplion and Norwich were the two important places in my imagination. They each had a sacred quality in my inner life.

A person traumatized in childhood interacts with my dream

This topic "Inner Journeys to Sacred Places" has been a theme of workshops I have been giving. The way that people take up inner work around this theme shows its vitality for healing. In one workshop I described an exercise to a group. It was a combination of the sand tray method developed by Dora Kalff[10] and the play which Jung did with stones and sand on the beach of the Zurichsee.[11] I asked the workshop group to think of an inner place they had gone in their dreams or in outer reality, which had about it a quality of fascination and mysterium tremendum. I then invited them to go to the beach to bring out this place in living stones and sand and three dimensional construction.

What took place for those who participated was truly amazing. Not all the group members participated at the beginning but most came along later to see and hear about what the others had constructed and, in some cases, to actually enter some of the spaces which were large enough to hold the whole group.

One person in the group constructed a giant mandala with stones. It could be seen clearly from the bluff above the beach. It had a powerful effect on other members of the retreat center who were not part of our workshop. One woman described what she saw the same evening that the giant encircling chain of stones had been laid there. She said the heron, whose habitat was this little section of coast, came and stood in the very center of the great mandala. All week, other members of the workshop watched as the upcoming tides covered these rocks, only to see them reemerge in their pristine form.

On the beach, I constructed in sand, rocks and shells a place I go in my dreams. I call it the shrine of Norwich. There in the evening as the waves lapped the nearby shore, I described to the group the process of this outer construction as it had unfolded. A tiny rivulet of sea water, seeking to connect itself with the sea after being left on the higher beach tide by the vanishing tide, became in imagination, my covered corridor. This I went up entering on my right, the medieval hospital. Constructing the walls with shells, I had then used small rectangles of flotsam wood to make the beds of this tiny place. There, too, was a bed for the Great Physician "who is also sick." Across the way I had constructed the chapel which was connected to the hospital. Rock walls formed the sides. A flat stoned, high altar was at the end. I could imagine candle-light filling this place. On the far right the chapel merged with a cave where prehistoric bones lay in the ancient dust. What surprised me most from this process of actually making a dream into an outer, sculpted form was this: the hallway from the hospital now led directly into the chapel. Healing and a sense of the sacred were in my awareness becoming more intimately connected.

One of the women of the group chose to work with me in the group a day or so later. In it she brought out some of her childhood trauma. During the day afterwards she couldn't move; she did no more than lie on the outer circle of the group, next to the wall of the building. On the last evening of the workshop, she said she was going to bring a drawing she had made; she requested that no one make any comments. She had said earlier that day how it had affected her to see my hospital with its doorway and floor plan lying on an axis with the doorway to the chapel. She said she knew her soul was sick.

The next morning, which was the last meeting of the workshop, I stood in the middle of the floor holding her drawing. It had just been shown to me. A little earlier she had said she felt things lifting, becoming lighter (she felt herself moving away from the childhood traumatic experiences which had tormented her whole life). Standing there in the middle of the room, as people danced and moved to music, I realized this picture of a terrified person amidst terrifying events, had indeed been transformed. I realized that to be of assistance like this was significant, for me.

The woman told me later that an altar had been made out of her picture the night before, after the session. One person had strewn a scarf all around it. Another person had put flowers there, etc. On her way home she stopped with friends at a motel. There she had a chance to do her own sand painting with stones. In one construction, a baby lay with stones around it, protected by the temenos or container in the form of a mandala or circle. Another construction of hers was most remarkable. There the outer stones took the shape of a winged cape with its hood rising as a triangle. Inside were many rocks. The child, she said, represented by these rocks, was in the cloak (and protection) of an angel.

During our individual work after the workshop she said she feared I would hate her. I said I did not hate her. I added that it could be important to let that part represent itself. She said there were two parts, and she was confused between them. One part was the feeling I hated her. The other part felt connected to me. I asked if she felt safer if she thought I hated her. She said yes. Then she said that in the past the way she protected herself was to go away where things were different. Letting herself be close to me (not being hated by me) was moving on from the isolation and dissociation caused by her childhood trauma.

Exercises

In doing inner work which may take you quite deep, it is important that you allow yourself enough time and space. If you are ready, let's go.

Exercise 1

Think of a place which for you has fascination, even mysterium tremendum. Some places are associated with creative inner work for us. Jung writes:

> In Bollingen I am in the midst of my true life. I am most deeply myself. Here I am, as it were, the "age-old son of the mother." That is how alchemy puts it, very wisely, for the "old man," the "ancient," whom I had already experienced as a child, is personality #2, who has been and always will be. He exists outside time and is the son of the maternal unconscious. In my fantasies he took the form of Philemon, and he comes to life again at Bollingen.[12]

Joseph Campbell speaks of a sacred place in incubation of creativity.[13] This suggests another exercise for you.

Exercise 2

1) Is there a special, even sacred space you go in your dreams? Or is there an outer place where you are truly alive?

2) Go there now in your active imagination.

3) Meditate, follow your process, allowing the natural shifting of channels to occur until a surprise comes.

4) You may want to turn the surprise into writing, sketching, sculpture, or movement. If so, you may want to continue with the below.

More information on working with inner processes:

a) If you are hearing and writing:
Just let the words come,
the more spontaneous, the better,
don't do much judging;
allow yourself to be carried away
by the sounds;
just go with the rhythm;
allow unusual images,
things that don't make sense;
allow things others could judge;
don't stop until it feels complete.

b) If you are seeing and drawing:
let your hand do the work;
even hold the crayon sideways, flat;
again don't judge;
let yourself be surprised by the colors which come to you from within;
don't try to control shapes and reason things out,
instead, let them burst upon you as if you were having the feeling of making a mistake;
let it happen;
don't direct the work to please anyone.

11

c) If you are moving or dancing:
find a spot where you can move freely;
let yourself go;
you can come back to what comes to you, later;
perhaps take a friend or turn on an imaginary video camera;
when the work is going on, remember no movement is too subtle;
let yourself be guided;
if you shift to auditory or visual, follow this;
let it come back to kinesthetic;
don't be afraid of looking crazy;
after the experience make some choreographic sketches;
ask yourself then, where did you stop?

d) If expression is in the relationship channel:
pick someone to work with who is like the problematic person
you have in mind;
ask that person to be like the problematic person;
talk to him or her about the person so he or she can play the
part, giving guidance for the role;
give feedback (yeah, that's like it, no . . .);
practice being in touch with yourself while you are relating to
the person;
go back and forth between being the problematic person part
and the part with which you identify;
give yourself time-outs to check on what you are feeling or
what is coming to you.

e) If your idea is something which involves the world channel:
set down your ideas about your idea or image of doing
something in the world;
think of the people you would like to gather (if any) to help you
with this idea;
let the possibilities come to you without judging them,
initially, even if they seem vague;
imagine that your friends in this venture are present;
let out all the stops;
tell them what this idea is going to do;

ask each of them what you want of them;
tell them what you are willing to do;
figure out what you can do if the response to this idea is even
greater than you imagine;
find out who your inspirer is and dialogue with that factor.

Exercise 3

The Journey. Is there a journey you especially like to take, perhaps a journey where you feel very much yourself? Take the journey now. Again observe and follow the switches of the channels of information as they happen. Follow the surprise. When it feels complete, you may want to discuss your experience with a friend or partner.

Exercise 4

A further exercise involves making the sacred place in the plastic arts or in sculpted material. Using the sand of a beach or the soft earth of a garden, make your own sand tray. Build your sacred inner space with sand, stones, pieces of bark, etc. Allow the process to unfold. Then, if you wish, tell a friend, bringing them into your sculpted sacred inner space. Please remember this admonition as you work on your dreams or other material from the psyche: ". . . for centuries (persons) had esteemed the fundamentals of the old French PELERINAGE—a journey to a sacred spot, could bring the devotee some supernatural benefit or dispensation."[14] May it be so with you.

Maybe it is always important to bring your inner journeys to sacred places into the outer world, as I did at the workshop, when the container (temenos), the time, and the place are right. In the epilogue, I shall share a journey I made through dreams into the meaning, for me, of the Grail.

two

Psychological Transformation Arising from the Transpersonal: the Experience of a Modern Nun

Reflecting upon the emerging spiritual problem of the modern person, C. G. Jung said that the body would be one of the new frontiers. He meant the body as it manifests a unitary reality with psyche, inner life and spirit.

Jung draws upon the early church father, Clement of Alexandria, to show that these realms were not always split in Western, Christian culture. He speaks of spirit as "spiritual life," in modern terms. Referring to a drawing, he makes note of the spirit dwelling there. He continues: "The underlying symbolical thought is no doubt the same as the view developed in the Clementine Homilies, that πνευμα (spirit) and σωμα (body) are one in God."[1]

Process Workshops

The process workshops often involve people in a deeper connection with their own spirituality and religious roots. But this happens as we work with dreams, body symptoms, and relationship problems. The modern person—whether religious in the usual sense, or not—can gain from process and Jungian psychology, a deep appreciation for the healing process. By this I mean the transformation arising from the transpersonal.

Years ago I chose graduate studies in the field of psychology and religion. It has been my work and area of study ever since. People, many of whom had little or no outward link to religion, have found in process work a "religious attitude" of awe and mystery toward the greater forces in the soul which motivate life.

I would like to share with you something of what I have found in the work in which I have participated. It has been made clear to me that the space of inner healing connects with the world. In my own life my early motivation to be close to the souls of people has come home to rest in my workshops. There, the love I felt early in life for people in their essence, now finds a viable outlet. And the hope, and even yearning, I had for people's fulfillment, comes out as I see people grow and move.

I shall try to convey this to you through the story of a nun, a very remarkable lady, who got closer in her process work to that inner spirit which motivates. This wonderful lady had had three surgeries for three different primary cancers.

The Nun's Experience

The woman was in constant pain not only from her bouts with cancer but from the complications arising from the treatment. Also, it was as if the financial problems of the innovative project which she had designed in an Eastern city and now led, created unbelievable tension in her body. Not to live in the face of such uncertainty and trial would to her have meant boredom and mediocrity. "I want to get out of this physical pain," the woman said at the beginning. Yet the life of her project—which involved the welfare and expansion of many other people—seemed to depend on her living on the financial edge. She said that was not all of it and that if she didn't live on this edge, she would need to create another edge. Yet her pain was so great that she said in order to escape, she had at times thought of desperate measures which she might have effected if it had not been for the support of my colleague who worked regularly with her.

We were working with her utilizing process work. She asked if she could perhaps experience the pain in another channel of information. We tried that. Then my colleague said, "I am willing to go to the edge of 'the envelope' with you." The client had previously said this is where the human meets God. The woman laid back on the floor, and my colleague gently pulled her neck and asked if she was a little more comfortable. "A little," she said.

15

The woman said she needed a little time. She was entering a deeper space. Then she was at the place where, as she said, the human meets the divine. Then she said softly that her sister, deceased some twenty years previously, was with her. The woman and her sister began a dialogue; the sister had died of cancer as a young woman in her twenties. The two sisters were talking. Each expressed curiosity and wonder at the other's experience: one in life, and one in death. Each person had some poignant questions to ask of herself; the one alive asked why she had not gone on to join her deceased mother and sister. And the deceased sister likewise expressed regret at taking the direction of an early death. She seemed to want to support her sister in remaining alive and living her life; the deceased sister seemed to value living more highly that dying.

Now the sister seemed to give our client instruction. The woman had begun to feel tight over her head. And in the deceased sister's dialogue with her, the sister asked her to form the light into a sphere. This the woman did. Then the sister told her to bring the sphere of light down into her head. Now the woman's breathing had quietened, and she was fully in an altered state of consciousness. The sphere of light was in her head for a while, and then the sister asked her to bring the light down into her body. The woman was absorbed in this phenomenon. My colleague began moving her hands over the downward lines of her body a few inches above her actual torso and I followed suit, my hands above those of my colleague. Then the sister's voice asked our client to let her use the light to take out from the bottoms of her feet all the pain which was in her body.

After some time the sister asked her to regroup the light and bring it again up through her body. She asked her to have the sphere of light in her head. At this point the sister suggested a procedure which in my knowledge of meditation practices, seemed dangerous to our client, and I intervened. The particular procedure was averted, the woman remained in a trance, and the light formed itself into a sphere above the top of her head.

While the light was again coming up the woman's body, she and her sister had a dialogue about the project: the project seemed

16

almost a matter of life and death and that her own bodily processes had become in her illnesses an almost unbearable pain. The sister told her it didn't matter if the project lived or died; what mat-
tered was that it was infused with light—the light, she was told,
was God's love. Now the woman wanted to bring this sphere of
light over each of OUR heads. And I placed my head near her
hands as they made their sweep in our direction, her eyes remaining closed. And as her hands cupped over my head something
important happened to me (which I shall report later).

The woman brought her hands over the head of my colleague
in much the same manner as with me. The woman then asked for
my help. I counseled her to complete this conversation with her
sister. The two said their farewells for that moment. The woman
expressed amazement to her sister about how simple it had seemed
to contact her. The woman asked her sister to tell her (deceased)
mother that she loves her. The sister objected that her mother
already knew that. Then the woman asked her to tell the mother
anyway. The two parted. The pain had been gone. Then as the
woman returned from her altered state of consciousness, the pain
came back. She wanted to discuss the matter, but my colleague
and I dissuaded her from this at that moment. The meeting of the
three of us, which at the client's request had begun in prayer, had
to end due to time commitments.

The woman and I were riding afterwards in the same car to our
various destinations. But I took over at the wheel. She sat in the
seat at my side. Again she wondered if she should turn to an intel-
lectual understanding of what had happened. I said I would try to
be open to doing or not doing that, depending on what happened;
then I became aware that I would share what the work had meant
to me.

I told the woman that when she in her trance had placed her
cupped hands over my head, I had felt the completion of an unre-
solved experience of fourteen years before. There was no longer
any hesitation, resistance or fear. Something extraordinary happened, a process now fourteen years old, had completed itself.

As we drove in the car, the woman said she had never felt so
relaxed. She, who was very verbal by nature, often lapsed into

silence. She then agreed with me that it was important that she had not tried to drive so soon after such a big experience. She had had a mystical experience, she said, which was on par with one other mystical experience which had happened about six months before this time. She said she thought she could skip the pain medication that evening, something she hadn't been able to do for months prior. As of the time of this writing, she has remained off pain medication. She said she was looking forward to going to work the next day. She laughed at her previous perception that her world was to see the bills were paid in her creative and precarious project. Now she said her work was all about the love of God suffusing the reality of her project.

There was another part of this work for me. It was the dream which followed that same night. In the dream I had the courage to bodily throw a man who was threatening to be inappropriate with a soul figure of mine. I did this in spite of his obvious skill in martial arts, and I prevented the soul from being offended. Then, I had to escape the thugs who were likely to attack me simply because I was around him. This I did. The experience of working with the woman on the day before presented me with a spiritual view of life. I could not permit a demeaning and disrespectful shadow attitude to overcome my soul's new attitude.

The woman's primary process was to identify with living on the edge. For her this meant working with a very creative and valuable project, which required all her ingenuity to keep it afloat. It seemed her stress over this and even her pain were worthwhile; moreover, to her, they seemed to signify living on the edge.

My colleague and I helped her enter the process of being on the edge of "the envelope." This was a bigger edge than living with the tension of the financial security surrounding her very valuable project. As her process unfolded, she experienced her definition of the edge of "the envelope" as the frontier where the human meets the divine. Her experience there recast her understanding of what it means to live on the edge.

In the voice of her sister had come a recognition that it didn't ultimately matter whether her project lived or failed but what did matter was whether it was filled with God's light, a quality of

God's love. Her job wasn't to be identified then with the struggle to pay the bills but with the deeper essence of helping to bring the quality of divine love into the project (the secondary process). With that awareness, she relaxed, as did her pain. She no longer needed to identify with it. Her secondary process was to realize her essence, behind her outward form as a religious person struggling in life; her essence was to go deeper into the mystery and meaning of the frontier of "the envelope" and to bring that renewed meaning into the world through her life.

Let us say that there is in many of us a part like "the holy sister" who is also a real person living in the real world. The "holy sister" part teaches me in my exposure to it that the world is not just what we see. The transpersonal part, which her deeper experience represented, actually is capable of transforming reality as we know it, including such aspects as physical pain. These experiences often take place in the field in which I have been privileged to work. I, like the people with whom I am working, feel I am transformed in the process we are sharing. I so deeply respected the nun and all she was trying to do with her life, under circumstances which would be extremely trying for almost anyone. I regard her as a great human being.

Theoretical Background

It is important to present some theoretical formulations which touch upon this book. In a special series on evaluation and treatment of pain, Larry E. Beutler of the University of Arizona College of Medicine, and his colleagues, write of the subject of pain and depression. After surveying segments of the literature, they suggest that when interpersonal anger is inhibited over a prolonged time, this may correlate with chronic pain, depression and susceptibility to disease. They go on to speak of blocked emotional experience coinciding with stress, which may be associated with deactivation of helpful natural killer cells, which fight disease, and natural pain analgesics of the body. These authors argue for the value of certain psychotherapeutic methods which unblock the emotions under specific favorable circumstances. They cite studies of Hokanson and Burgess (1962) and Hokanson and Shetter (1961) and bring out among other points the following: "These circumstances typically focused on the subjects' expectation that the expression of anger would have some positive influence on those around them."[2] I draw a conclusion analogous to this last point: it is that physical pain is more bearable when the subject experiencing it can see that it has a meaning beyond that individual's own life. Knowing that one's suffering in illness has some meaning to others and that it is not just an individual matter, seems to have an effect upon the pain.

C. G. Jung gives us some basic postulates which unite psyche and body and psyche and world. These form the underlying hypotheses of our discussion. In the famous filmed interviews of Jung by Richard S. Evans made in 1951, Jung spoke passionately about the importance of the psyche or the inner world of the human being. He said: "The world today hangs by a thin thread, and that thread is the psyche of man."[3]

Jung writes: "A wrong functioning of the psyche can do much to injure the body, just as conversely a bodily illness can affect the psyche; for the psyche and body are not separate entities, but one and the same life."[4]

He continues:

Since psyche and matter are contained in one and the same world, and moreover are in continuous contact with one another and ultimately rest on irrepresentable, transcendental factors, it is not only possible but fairly probable, even, that psyche and matter are two different aspects of one and the same thing.[5]

In another place, Jung states: "There is no difference in principle between organic and psychic formations. As a plant produces its flowers, so the psyche created its symbols."[6]

This is all very similar to Arnold Mindell's sense of global processes. Mindell's school of psychology, process work, as this school is called, links up what is happening to the individual, or group and world. Mindell writes: "Ideally, process work focuses on the endurable unit and the channels which are used in a given moment. At any time, this unit might break up into smaller, indivisible units or unite with others to form a larger one."

The example which comes to mind is of a young man I knew when I taught in Friends World College. He came down with a virus. The virus had to do with his fear that he would not be able to do what he wanted to do in life. As we worked with his dreams, we discovered his edge to really live his own personal myth. He had been told as a young person that he must work hard, harder than others or he would not succeed. At the same time he had been told, if he worked too hard and did not care for himself, then he would fall sick, maybe even die. Since he had nearly died as a teenager from undiagnosed pneumonia, he felt beyond any reason that one sickness could be his death. He recalled this prolonged illness as comprised of time after time of feeling better only to discover that the disease held on, and that the medicines and doctors didn't work. The virus he had as a college student could have gone deeper and deeper as he took to his bed in one of those cold, old houses without central heat in England.

He was getting no better. Then something began to change in his psyche. He began to talk to me about a conviction he had that . . . but let me back up. We worked on this dynamic mentioned above. He came to see that he was in the grip of a belief that only if he tried harder would he succeed, not only succeed but survive. He was both more sensitive and talented than the average person. But some well-meaning person, seeing his sensitivity, feared for him, and he picked this up as a process.

This broke when I told him what one of my teachers had told me—"you have to leave some room for God"—as a corrective to trying to arrange everything in the course of one's life. The second point was the discovery by him that the voice which said he would get sick if he worked too hard was a negative dream figure. It coincided with his edges he was facing that spring in his student project—parts of his belief system that he wouldn't be able to do certain things if they involved conflicts with others. Finally, his fear that he could not get well, was a distrust of the processes of the body to heal itself. He needed to trust more but that came in the conviction I mentioned earlier: it was that he was not more important than anyone or anything else that was ailing. He was genuinely hoping something would happen for all people and the earth, along the lines of Julian of Norwich: "All is well, and all manner of things are well, and all manner of things are well."[8]

Thinking of the bigger picture, the grid uniting all energies and particles, all people and places, he of course did get better. And not only did his virus slip away. In the larger vision he saw what he had always wanted to do in this life; he contacted what Jung called his personal myth. The conflicts he had imagined to working with certain other people became doorways into other, opposite type processes in himself, where he could grow in directions he had always rejected.

What is staggering about this is that he lost his fear, or a lot of it, for a young man.

These statements and stories I hope will unite for the reader the concepts of psyche with the body, and with healing. Healing of the parts in the individual is connected to healing in the group and world spheres.

Jung adds:

> Again, no psychological fact can even be exhaustively explained in terms of causality alone; as a living phenomenon, it is always indissolubly bound up with the continuity of the vital process, so that it is not only something evolved but also continually evolving and creative.[9]

To see so-called events as processes, processes which may continue to unfold, is the perspective of process work. As Mathew Fox writes: "Psychologist C. G. Jung confessed that [Meister] Eckhart offered him the 'key' to opening up the way to grasp what liberation means in a psychological context."[10]

Wrote Jung:

> The art of letting things happen, action through non-action, letting go of oneself, as taught by Meister Eckhart, became for me the key opening the door to the way. We must be able to let things happen in the psyche. For us, this actually is an art of which few people know anything. Consciousness is forever interfering . . . [11]

My Role

These reflections cause me to wonder at my own role, when I work with people, and the place of symptoms in my life and the lives of my clients. A disease is also a psychological process with an inner message, telling us how we can live and what we can do and not do. [12] It forces us to negotiate with our inner powers. For ultimately the power lies there in the archetypes which are behind our personal meaning and which impact our healing and health.

I cannot take on the healing of all who come across my path. I must take my new lodging by the ocean, where I look out upon the unconscious. I must leave the disease in the bodies of those who bring it to me, where it can work its own process of renewal like the pillar which contains the regenerative powers of Osiris. I can only be in touch with that same miracle in my life, where the Great Physician renews and heals. Those who come to me may sense that when present. I must do no more than one could do with a figurative or symbolic disease (following the process as it unfolds). Then I am in touch with what afflicts and also heals and who sets the limits on my life. It is a matter of transferring the burden from the ego, where it has erroneously been placed, to the self.

If we look deep within our lives, perhaps we can come to an understanding of emotional hurt as well as pain. I was trying to do this recently. I wondered how I could be around a certain individual and still not be hurt. This question put me in touch with the part that cannot be hurt. That part in me is the compassion and healing which has its source in the gods and goddesses. To my way of thinking, this source survives death.

Psyche and World

The world of healing is a great place for people to again become in touch with the great powers of life which go beyond our individual identities. This healing is so important not only for us as individuals, but for our world. The world suffers from a loss of appreciation and awe for these great factors which give rise to well-being.

Jung spoke of these great factors as being part of the self, or god—image in the person. He spoke of the god-image, not attempting as a psychologist to make statements of what this power might or might not be beyond that. But he was quite clear as to the effects of the loss of that sense of the underlying forces of life. William Kennedy quotes Jung's statement: "The destruction of the God-image is followed by the annulment of the human personality." [13] Kennedy goes on to extract from Jung's writings that when ". . . the totality symbol, the organizing factor in the psyche . . . no longer functions . . . you have . . . the personality . . . split up . . . " This leads to the mass man and "confusion and disorientation." [14]

And when this annulment of these individual personalities takes place on a massive scale, as it has in our day, there are very great problems, indeed. When the underlying forces of life which Jung calls the "superior dominants," are treated as if they did not exist, they exert their power over life autonomously, unconsciously and often destructively. For example, when the energy for inner, spiritual life is not lived at all, it can flood the instinctual, biological realm with too much energy.

In his letter of September 14, 1960 to Miguel Serrano, Jung states the necessity of ". . . a new realization of our dependence upon superior dominants." He had already pointed out that, "As we have largely lost our Gods, we are in a similar predicament to Germany in the Twenties." But, Jung adds, ". . . we are apt to undergo the risk of a further, but this time worldwide, Wotanistic experiment. This means mental epidemy and war." [15] The Dalai Lama writes: "With the ever-growing impact of science on our lives, religion and spirituality have a greater role to play in reminding us of our humanity." [16]

In summary, Jungian psychology has these contributions to make to the question of healing. Jung discusses the centering process as the equivalent of the healing process. The very formulation of wholeness with which Jung has been associated is related etymologically to healing. The quality of balance or union of oppo-

sites, Jungian psychology finds as characteristic of early Greek formulations of medicine and philosophy.

Jung was interested more in finality than causality, and credited events with having this significance of telos, purpose and meaning. Jung even formulated reflection, as an instinct. That word
implies connections to meaning.

In process work, we allow the symptom to evolve, as a process.
This is very close to the ancient Greek expectation that "He who
wounded will cure." Or as Arnold Mindell had formulated it: "A
disease may be its own healing process." [17] Process work carries this
forward to regard dreams, body symptoms and relationship problems as more than difficulties to be overcome; they may also be
experienced as pathways to fulfillment, or wholeness. This has a
parallel in Buddhism. According to the Lo Jong teachings
(Thought Transformation), when a person becomes skillful
enough to enter the very heart of the sympton, "the remedy releas-
es itself."

Exercise:

Take a few minutes to imagine a figure from your dreams or
real life who inspires you. [18]

Who is the inspired one in you?

What is this figure like?

How do you become when creative inspiration is your urge?

Do you sit down after a relationship experience and write?

Do you walk by a stream or in the desert and start your inner
dialogue?

Are you working after the manner of dreams: writing them
down, folding them, walking with them, cherishing them?

What are your ways?

Do you make tears, cry "cries"?

Do you feel pains?

How does your creative inspiration come to you?

Perhaps you don't want to create, don't feel you can create;
who is the figure that tells you or makes you feel non-creative?

Process work proposes to follow this process of natural healing
through an understanding of primary and secondary process and

the switches among the channels of information with which a person perceives her or his experience. Follow these processes and switches as they actually take place as you contact the one who inspires. And write down your experiences afterwards.

The Most Real

Life is a poem it is true
you think you can stick words on it,
life the bearer has you
there are no words for the very it.

Anger comes parading in
and rage powders her face,
both think to have substance therein
yet have no solid place,

As does the feeling of fear,
it runs at the first chance,
nor does it reside in the tear,
that which is nearer to dance.

Mindful I was of mind
not thoughts so much as images sped
of eye, then ear, a kind
of fluidity my soul led.

Becoming, nature displays
it somewhere in process between
the stone statement and maze,
beyond forms, unseen

When a bird flies in one
window and out another
one can easily mistake
the air of the house as the most real.

three

Centering & Healing . . .
the Journey into the Mandala

There are many ways of contacting the center of one's being. We shall consider some time-honored ways and then the particular contributions of process and Jungian psychology.

In my experience, the strongest possible approach to inner work is a combination of:

1. process work and process meditation;
2. active imagination;
3. Jungian dream interpretation (here applied to centering and circumambulation around the personality's center);
4. contemplation, inner work, and relating these to outer reality.

Also important is creativity in finding the personal relevance of inner work, and of appreciation and awe toward inner processes. We shall briefly discuss these ways not only theoretically, but with a view to making them available to your use in inner work.

Inner work will, over time, involve one with one's center. A definition, for me, of ultimate centering, is enlightenment. A friend of mine speaks of our activities, such as writing a book, as useful but lacking full significance, unless one is enlightened. Many Tibetan Buddhist teachers admonish their students to believe that enlightenment is possible for those individuals within this lifetime. I believe it is valuable for all of us to live as if it is possible to achieve wholeness within our lifetimes. Inner work is a discipline for working toward one's full realization.

Visual Inner Work

All over the world in all epochs, individuals have experienced an image of the center of their being; this has often come in the form of the mandala. The mandala might have been a dorje (symbol of skillful means or compassion) in the midst of four walls with four gates, surrounded by a circle (mandala, in Sanskrit); or, it could have been Christ's face with the four-part cross behind him surrounded by a circle; or it could have been a Navaho sand painting in which a person sits, awaiting healing. The mandala is a manifestation of a universal centering tendency in the human being which arises naturally from the psyche.

The similarity of this and many other symbols across cultural boundaries was datum for Jung's positing of an objective psyche or collective unconscious. Indeed, we find that today the mandala appears spontaneously in people's drawings and imaginations in time of stress, in people who may have no familiarity with the formal idea of the mandala. More information on the mandala will appear later in this chapter.

Jung speaks in his *Memories, Dreams, Reflections* of the great value of painting or sculpting one's fantasies and dreams. He states that he could not have otherwise become in touch with their messages which were subliminal and beyond words. During and after the process of inner work through drawing and sculpture, feelings and words come. I myself have been able to work out certain things this way which I do not believe would have been possible in other ways. Often, for me, an inestimable feeling of well-being followed the effort to draw, paint or sculpt the visions of an awe-inspiring dream.

Those who use visual work may know that it is very important to draw in such a way that the conscious mind may be released from total control. It is suggested that if you use acrylic crayons, for example, that you hold them flat in your fingers rather than relying on the point. This renders less possible the attempt to pinpoint a subject, and allows things to emerge from the more formless flat sweeps of color, as imagination freely accompanies the work of the hands.

Auditory Inner Work

Fantasies and dream-like phenomena can also come in the auditory channel of information. Attentiveness to sound, in this instance, can become the object of one's awareness.

Music would be one example from the province of sound. Isaac Stern speaks of ". . . the great power of music to touch the soul . . . to make the ephemeral immortal." Stern continues: "Only discipline frees the artist to let imagination take wing."[1] The same can be said about inner work and applying active imagination, process meditation, and contemplation.

Let us consider some forms of centering through audition. In his concept of "active imagination" Jung really developed the use of the verbal and auditory channels as means of centering. In this approach one may have an inner dialogue with a dream figure, for example. However, active imagination is not limited to the auditory channel of information but may include seeing, moving and dancing, and sculpting in a medium with plasticity. What characterizes active imagination is active engagement with fantasy material. In one of her books, Barbara Hannah gives a complete description of working with active imagination.[2]

Centering through Feeling

A further channel of information which can be utilized for centering is proprioception, or feeling in the body. For some, the body can be the subject of awareness. Just experiencing what one is really experiencing in one's feelings, can be a form of centering. Picking the body is like picking one channel of information from the many which are available from process work. A little later we shall discuss process mediation which can begin at any point, with what is happening in one's body, or vision, or hearing, etc. Some of people's deepest experiences come from going further into their feelings, allowing themselves to experience the feelings more. Once one has had such a deep body experience, one can access it again later as a point around which centering can reoccur.

Moving and Centering

In the area of body movement, it is again possible to become aware of the center of one's being. Examples from the phenomenology of world experience would be Tai Chi, prostrations in

29

Tibetan Buddhist practice, walking meditation from the Theravadin traditions, and so on.

Process work often calls attention to movements which are not completed or which are abrupt. Very slight movements can be worked with in a minute way.[3] Process work also involves other channels of awareness: relationship and world. In the relationship channel I am engaged with another person whether that person is present or in my imagination. In the world channel synchronicities occur, acausal connections between inner and outer events. And channels of information may be composite, for example, vision occurring with movement.

We will now be turning to the relationship of these different channels of information to each other and how they flow from one to another.

Process Meditation

Process meditation is fluid meditation. There are usually three steps. In this form of meditation you first find what channel of information (e.g. visual, auditory, etc.) to which your attention is being given in that moment. You then amplify the signal in that channel of information. Allow to happen the changes or switches of channels of information which occur naturally—for example, from visual to hearing—until you come upon something which is a surprise to your consciousness. When that happens, follow closely what unfolds from that point.[4]

Process meditation draws upon the information which might be available in any specific perceptual channel such as feeling. It combines this with a facility to allow the shifts which seem to want to happen to take place, shifts from one information channel to another, from feeling to seeing, for example. Therefore in any one period of meditation, contemplation or centering one might be in several or even many channels of information.

This description of process meditation is a key to how process work takes place and works. It applies not only to meditation but to therapy. In both cases, one follows the shifts from one channel of information to another.

Another dynamic also characterizes process work as therapy. It involves awareness of primary and secondary processes. Primary process concerns what an individual may be identifying with. Secondary processes are less known and powerful phenomena in the background which although appearing to be problematic and edgy may promise the wider fulfillment of the person. We saw in the last chapter the manifestation of primary and secondary process in the nun's experiences.

I want to describe for you how the creative process unfolds in a young man. In this you will see how process work follows switches of information channels such as visual, auditory, kinesthetic and proprioceptive. The person talked of a childhood trauma. He gave a signal. I saw his eyes looking at a distance. I had ideas of how to work with it. I asked him what he was seeing. A new lining was forming in his stomach, where there had been holes and leaks before, where the presence of mind had gone out. He heard the words, "balm, salve." (The process had switched to the auditory channel of information.)

He then recalled there was the lungfish which becomes leathery when there is no water, but later the lungfish is dislodged from the fissure in the hardened clay, when the water softens its surroundings, and the leathery creature, formerly in a ball, becomes transformed into a sleek fish. Then there was more seeing on his part. The tiles on the childhood home floor, he mentioned. Looking closer, he saw them bathed in light . . . further container of his childhood experience and essence, a floor emitting light, bringer of childhood knowledge of self into a situation formerly felt as dissipating his energies. His hands tapped six beats, four times. Poetry is heavy, mind is beyond his grasp, he said.

"Were there words to the beat?" I asked him.

"I want no more of holes that leak," he said.

"Poems are like that," I said. His words with natural rhythm continued. I recalled that Shakespeare's audiences benefitted from hearing the inner thoughts of the characters, spoken with poetry which seemed to flow from an inner source.

In my office setting with this young poet I felt: I am an audience, and I am in awe of his speech. There was a note of wonder as we both experienced the creative. The young man went on to really find his voice in poetry and his creative spirit in his life as a young father and husband.

Jung speaks of ". . . those dark regions of the psyche from which all human achievements ultimately spring, whether they be artistic creations or nervous disorders."[5] With many people I meet, the choice seems to be between those great processes, one destructive, the other following one's life myth.[6]

Jung's Interpretation of Dreams of the Center

Jung describes a series of dreams of a modern, scientifically trained individual in which the image of the center appears and reappears in a series of several hundred dreams.[7]

He utilizes the imagery of alchemy for a deeper understanding of the imagery of the circle and as a comparative process to the one taking place in the modern scientist's dream life. The essence of alchemy is a centering process, according to Jung. This is also the essence of many meditative practices.

Jung shows that in the process of centering, Western and Eastern approaches to inner life are comparable and compatible. Let us look at Buddhist tangka paintings for the purposes of illustration. There is often a great circle divided by four parts. Within the outer circle, central to it, is a center. Sometimes there are four walls with four gates leading toward this center. In the center may be Buddha or Tara, a female Buddha. The Western equivalent to this pattern may be the rose, or Christ, or Christ in the uterus of the Virgin.

One's dreams will follow this imagery of the center if one follows and relates with consciousness to one's dreams when the individuation process is taking place. This is, indeed, the pattern Jung found in the series of dreams he considered of the scientifically trained individual mentioned above.

In addition to the pictorial representation of the center or centering process, there is the act of circumambulation. As already suggested above, what is in the center of the mandala or circle is a god or goddess, or an aspect of the deity . . . the highest value.

All these could be viewed as representations of the self, the total realization of the personality. Jung writes: "As manifestations of the unconscious processes, the dreams rotate or circumambulate round the center, drawing closer to it as amplifications increase in distinctness and scope." Speaking again of the past series of dreams he studied, many of which contain images of the center, Jung continues: "The development of these symbols is almost the equivalent of a healing process." [8]

Contemplation

Contemplation is still another form of inner work. It requires that one be in a place where one can give concentration to one's experience. In contemplation, one lets the mind work around a basic human quality, for example, mortality. I think of how working with "the diamond body and reincarnation" (chapter four) grew out of such contemplation for me and also, how writing can be part of the contemplation process.

I think it is also possible for a dream or dream image to provide the focus of contemplation. While considering dream material in more depth, one can do a contemplative type of inner work on a dream image and utilize active imagination as well. This form of meditation is different from analyzing in a critical way or regressively looking for causes. Contemplation is allowing the energy to expand through imagination and application. Contemplation can bring great peace. Combining dream-work with contemplation and active imagination may lead to a new answer.

An Exercise of Circumambulation

Make a circle walking physically or figuratively around a center—something of high or highest value from your inner life. As you move or picture yourself moving, always have the center in your awareness. Picture this on an outward plane. There in the center of a great circle you are making as you walk, is the supreme value of your life. Some would express this center as your personal myth or the reason you have come into the world in this lifetime. So you are walking. All sorts of things come up: practical things, esoteric things; outer things, inner life; upper things and under things; masculine and feminine aspects. But remember, there is a center.

If you get to feeling hassled, stressed or unbalanced, remember where you are. All your activities take place around a central core. You can come back to it. Then you will be centered again. Your whole life, and mine, can be lived with that awareness of circumambulating the center. What does it mean to have a center to the personality? It is to come back again and again to the goal and the essence of one's being. All the inner controversies, the ceaseless dialogue, the worries, can be resolved by that.

In centering meditation, one may try to visualize the circulation of the light. One great image of it might be the light particles of the universe swirling in a circular pattern. Still another image might be the petals of a light flower flowing around its center as it is turned. Another symbol which appeared spontaneously for one person during her meditation was shafts of light which rose through the length of her body to emerge into a radial pattern at the head. I also recall the sphere of light which occurred in a vision to the woman described in chapter two. Finally, to still another person a cross shape appeared, golden in color, rotating and giving off reflections of light as the arms moved.

An Exercise in Process Meditation

You can start this exercise with writing, drawing, dancing, or with relationship or world work. Or you could begin with a dream, a symptom or a relationship problem. Follow the switches of channels when they occur in your work. For example, you may start writing inner dialogue (auditory) but find yourself moving (kinesthesia) which could become spontaneous dance, etc. When something comes as a surprise, follow that with all your energy until it becomes complete.

In summary, all the ways of inner work described in this chapter allow one to work on one's own. If you can work on you own, you will probably be able to cope with most any situation. You will be carrying your teacher with you. As processes unfold, the WOUND BECOMES THE PATHWAY TO CREATIVITY.

four

The Diamond Body
& the Centering Process

Virtually everyone is interested in the question of death, although some will assume that the question stops there. This chapter explores some more possibilities.

There are many ways to work with this question. One, it is a topic worthy of our contemplation, whether or not, as Jung suggests, we reach a satisfactory answer or image. Secondly, our dreams may tell us something about this subject. In this regard, Marie-Louise Von Franz's study is most valuable.[1] A third area is the study of comparative material, material which in certain cultures and epochs gives a comparison for modern subjective experience. We shall be considering data from each of these areas in the present chapter.

My own contemplation of death was completed for the present by a realization I received in contemplating one of Jung's experiences. On his stone in Bollingen, Jung writes of the self paradoxically as both mortal and belonging to the aeons. This sums up what I have been reaching for in my discussions of the diamond body. His idea and formulation clicked within me. I conclude: that which brought itself to life in me as a person and made my sense of conscious individuation possible, will appear again after my life and perhaps work its goal again, in another person. After this brief contemplation of mine, let us consider a dream.

A Personal Recollection of One who has Died & who is in my Dream

In my dream this morning there appeared to me the likeness of Bill—my mentor, dear friend, and person supporting me in life, in the beginning of my adulthood. He was so real to me in that moment, and in my meditation which preceded my writing this.

The remarkable thing about Bill in the dream (in real life, deceased nearly nine years ago at the time of my writing) was that he was completely revived, totally renewed in energy. The memories of him have started in my recent meditation and continue through this writing. The most recent memory was how he tried to be supportive to me when I was soon to be a new father. I can see his smiling, his light attitude at that tense moment for me, which was expressed on his face, and in his compassion.

In my meditation this morning I remembered that he carried the world on his shoulders; his life was important to the world situation. Life was a balance between these heavy responsibilities and an atonement to individual people, where he expressed joy and freshness.

He could carry with interest, things of a day-to-day nature in one part of himself, and let bigger things come through his actions, of which few besides himself were ever aware. He was a man who could talk to people, and they became enlisted in the bigger cause of which he was a part.

He made up for his mistakes in a big way, with imagination that few ever express. Perhaps this is what allowed him to live so fully in the face of the possible mistakes he could make.

I became aware in meditation that when one decides to live life, one is closer to death. It feels more like a possibility.

I remembered that when Bill and I were together in Greece, he would take his Sundays, at least till dinner time, to be by himself. I liken that to my knowledge now of how important is my meditation.

I have dreamed of Bill many times since his death. In one dream during the years shortly following his death, he seemed like a spirit following along with me in the shadows and connecting me with my spiritual beginnings in my hometown. Certainly, he as an image, is one of the representations of the self to me.

The dream today makes me wonder about the reality of death as we usually think of it. I wonder if he is still alive in some realm—a possibility. And he was realized as a human being in some ways. On another level, the dream says that what he represents is still alive, even alive in the psyche, and indeed what he represents does not die. It lives on in me and will live on, I trust, after my physical body is no longer here. I have had many other dreams which point to the contemplation of what death may mean. I invite you to recall your own dreams of this nature.

Comparative Material

Jung speaks of the Yellow Castle which was the subject of one of his paintings during the period of his confrontation with the unconscious between 1913-1927. In 1927 he painted the castle which, he said at the time, had a distinctively Chinese feeling about it. There was a synchronicity in that, for he soon received a Taoist-alchemical manuscript from Richard Wilhelm, the Chinese text known as *The Secret of the Golden Flower*. For Jung this made the vital link between the experiences of his inner journey and something in the outside world. It was the turning point for him. The isolation he had felt for nearly fourteen years was broken; he had found a link with the collective experience in this comparative material sent by Wilhelm.

Jung writes of the yellow castle which appears both in his painting and the Chinese text as "the germ of the immortal body." This is what links his experience with the present chapter.

Related to his yellow castle is his dream of Liverpool which occurred just prior to that painting. He reports that in his dream the city is laid out radially. He moves through a darkened, rainy and dirty city. But in its center on an island surrounded by a lake, a shaft of light is falling with majesty on a magnolia tree.[2]

Processes in the unconscious which produced the dream of Liverpool are related to those which resulted in the painting of the yellow castle. As I said earlier, this material becomes, step by step, our process of developing the topic of the immortal body. But there are still a few more links to be made. Jung writes under his picture of the yellow castle:

"A mandala as a fortified city with wall and moat . . . "[3]

Under Jung's production of this work are his words: ". . . the unseen bodies."[4]

As images of the collective psyche, the city and the immortal body are equivalent. When we dream of the city, are we dreaming likewise of that part of us that goes beyond this life? The city of Liverpool of Jung's dreams, like many dreams of the city, is really a mandala. This points to the fact that the centering process can in certain instances prepare a more transpersonal part of ourselves, which indeed challenges the borders of death itself.

The following dream of mine occurred the week I was preparing a workshop on the diamond body, centering and immortality. Often my dreams produce certain creative material around a topic I am considering. In this dream, my own process picked up the same theme as Jung's dream of Liverpool. In my dream, a shaft of light came into a rotunda with ringed tiers above; that rotunda was going to be the place of the workshop. Earlier in the dream, I saw a man who had light inside of him, as if it were preparing that part of him which goes on after life.

Now let's examine further the image of the city. The city lives on after our own individual lives are past. We contribute to the city, that is, to the human culture which is its heart, and that contribution lives on after us. We are the city, the city is us.[5] As such, the city represents for one thing the part of us which goes on after life, as we know it, is over.

The city is a representation of what we pass on. What we have been given at birth in human culture and the possibility of awareness, is also contained in this image. The city contains the library of human beings' collective experience, and this symbol of the city when it appears in our dreams points to all we have gained, or can gain from the experience of human history. These manifold experiences shape and are shaped by the archetypes of the collective unconscious. What is the link of the city as image, to the birth of our awareness? Here the city as an image is interchangeable with the divine spark, the spinthers, the light which inhabits the darkest matter (unconsciousness). This symbol comes up frequently in one form or another in my work with clients.

And here we have the link with timelessness, eternity. For what is of true wisdom, in which we live and move and have our being, goes on, like the city, after our lives have passed.

In *Psychology and Alchemy*, Jung states of this "city" of the inner world: "The symbolic city as center of the earth, its four protecting walls laid out in a square: [is] a typical TEMENOS."

He continues:

The square corresponds to the TEMENOS . . . , where a drama is taking place . . . The inside of the "golden flower" is a "seeding place" where the "diamond body" is produced. The synonymous term "the ancestral land" may actually be a hint that this production is the result of integrating the ancestral stages.[6]

Jung adds:

We have to conceive of these (fantasy) processes not as the immaterial phantoms we readily take fantasy-pictures to be, but as something corporeal, a subtle body . . . , semi-spiritual in nature.[7]

The great Buddhist, Nagarjuna, contributes a similar insight. The following statement is a commentary on the philosophy of this sage from the first century:

The Middle Way consists in the recognition that the complex system of personality is not absolute, that there is no element in it that forever remains the same, as well as no element in the system of personal life that ever perishes totally. It is essentially a process, not any unconditioned, substantial entity.[8]

If we are able to keep with the centering activity of the psyche, moving as it does around the image of the self (perhaps pictured in the city or other symbol), then in us may come to awareness the incorruptible substance which goes beyond this lifetime.

Reincarnation may be another comparative system to help us in the understanding of this possibility. That which belongs to the self reappears to orient another life. Here we may combine our philosophy with the insights of Buddhism. It is out of compassion that the enlightened Bodhisattva returns to human existence in order to assist others. The self reemerges in another life, another person.

"Sleeping and waking they are all the same, a mirror's edge into eternity." This statement came to me in a dream exactly as I have rendered it above. It seems to portend that I am on the right track in my efforts to connect the psyche's images of self, such as that of the city, with the idea of reincarnation. This has been my work and the object of my imagination, of recent days.

Images of the self as they appear in the psyche seem to portend the evolvement of something "incorruptible" as the alchemists put it. This adjective would seem to apply in the face of all states, including death.

Jung equated the individuation process with following, over time, the psyche's production of patterns representing the self. These were often presented in dreams in the forms of the mandala or other images of the centering process; likewise, the great work of the production and attention to these images was likened to the opus or lapis of the alchemists, with its goal of the incorruptible substance.

The individuation process is comprised of following with awareness the symbols of the self and becoming more integrative of all the contents of psychic life. This is equivalent of producing the "gold" or other symbol of the incorruptible substance. It does imply that this work produces something which is even beyond the powers of death to destroy.

How could this work? If the alchemists' work is combined with the Buddhist and Hindu theory of reincarnation, then perhaps there is a way. At the same time the Western adept is centering her being, she is doing something very akin to Eastern meditation—represented for example in the Tibetan Buddhist mandalas. Could it not be that the Western adept is in this process approaching something akin to the goal of Eastern meditation that is, enlightenment? Enlightenment has with it some choice about the form of reincarnation. An enlightened being, for example, may choose to return to the human realm and for the purpose of helping others, to also become totally aware.

Here compassion for all other beings has affected a psychic state or process. It is much as Jung has stated, that powerful active imagination builds up something akin to a psychic body or subtle body. Would the potentially enlightened Easterner not also be building something that transverses the wall of death in order to return as Bodhisattva in order to help enlighten other sentient beings? Might not the vehicle for that return of the Bodhisattva be something like the incorruptible substance, the goal of the alchemists' process and that of the modern person individuating? These latter processes are, after all, processes of meditation.

What is incorruptible is the psyche's capacity to be whole, once this is realized. Combined with compassion in the conscious choice to return to help others, this enlightenment substance of psychic life could pass the death barrier and return in a future incarnation, with the image of the self or wholeness close to awareness, so to speak. Such a person would be in a position to work from an image of psychic wholeness and balance, to live yet another life of compassionate assistance of others; that person would be in the image of the East, a Bodhisattva.

How does this tie in with the body? On the same night as my dream about reincarnation, I have a sense in a dream of needing to return to my body before I start doing things upon waking (which is in fact when the dream took place). In this state it feels like my body (above) is not yet in my body (below me). There is a sense that the part that rises up at the night, and travels, has its own body.

Perhaps this later body is figurative, representing a part of me which is not the same as my existence on earth in space and time. This could be yet another representation of the underlying *possibility* of forming a diamond body.

I find that Meister Eckhart's statement is similar to this intuition I just reported. D. J. Suzuki's comparisons of Meister Eckhart and Zen Buddhist philosophy are most enlightening; he quotes Eckhart from one of his sermons on poverty:

> . . . therefore, I am my own first cause, both of my eternal being and my temporal being. To this end I was born, and by virtue of my birth being eternal I shall never die. It

is of the nature of this eternal birth that I HAVE BEEN eternally, that I AM now, and SHALL BE, forever. What I am as a temporal creature is to die and come to nothingness, for it came with time and so with time it will pass away. In my eternal birth, however, everything was begotten. I was my own first cause as well as the first cause of everything else. If I had willed it, neither I nor the world would have come to be. If I had not been, there would have been no god. There is, however, no need to understand this. [9]

That something may go beyond this life—and there is reason to let our imagination and experience play with this—is suggested in a point Jung makes late in his life. "During the War," Jung said, "I saw men who had received brain wounds which paralyzed the functions of the cerebral cortex, and thus prevented them from having any sense of space or time. Nevertheless, they were still able to dream . . ." He said, "You know, of course, that a small child has no clearly defined sense of the Ego . . . If the physical Ego disappears at death, does that other Ego also disappear, that other one which had sent him dreams as a child?" [10]

On the night after I saw this statement and copied it here, I had a dream in which I came out of a threshold to think I would find my wife. It seemed like she was there, but actually there were two flowers in two pots, symbolic of our souls in another form; perhaps they emanated from that center which produced the dreams of our childhood.

My dream seemed to make its own commentary in support of Jung's statement. Perhaps as you follow the material and methods I have gathered here, you, too, will want to be aware of your own psyche's commentary on these inner journey to sacred places; this may, as we revolve closer and closer to our center, at the same time be healing.

Summary

If we recall that the essence of alchemy is centering, then perhaps Jung's statement will show its correlation with the diamond body and with symbols such as the city. In Chinese philosophy the mandala is the "Square Inch Field of the Square Foot House." It is said that the house means the Imperishable Body and the building up of that mandala means the building up of the Imperishable Body . . . the subtle body is the definite abode for what old philosophy would have called entelecha, the thing which tries to realize itself in existence.[11]

I shall end this chapter by telling how words and pictures burned in me as I sat by a fire and recalled the dream of the night before. It was that terrible, pregnant time just before the Gulf War. The second part of this poem, where I speak about a Greek priest, refers to seeing in the dream, the rift between life and death; I was seeing a scene similar to Rafael's painting of "The School of Athens," in which all the great philosophers, poets, and poetesses of antiquity, are gathered.

Revelations by the Fire

As the log opened
fire bright, candescence, flamed
there in the cave-like hearth
the brightest light
dios prepared to announce
its surprises in the world.

The worst news
dios might still turn 'round.
An intuition like this—
the hottest flame—
brings inside me, a child, and joy.

World's sufferings
beyond me,
I can't contain,
Only one big as world
can.

Dios, eternal in the flame
in the word
and in the heart
can
Kyrie Eleison.

Open hearth
open me
to what is newly
arising in me . . .

This the wise man
old and green
wearing moss on his sleeve
who met me in a dream,

Just before the crossing
where the road
widened past the wood,

And I knew
he had been preparing
some course for me
just by his Way,

What lay before me . . .
more, more Being like his,
more ripening,
his preparing,

I remembered the way
through a second wood
to the quiet garden
with the lily'd pond centre

To the place of learning
the Wise Old Man's school
where quiet is contained in knowledge
of the Self within.

The mystery is there
he's waiting in the woods,
fire ready to burn
child to be born.

By the crossing
before the step, I found
a wood growing,
a long staff

like the walking sticks
by Jung's door
opening into
the guide's house,

Woodsman, then like Jung,
the step beyond
opening
into the Greater Way.

Were I to tell you
of the favors dios gives
his children
you'd see the fire,
as these other dreams, too
dios gave to me:

The Greek priest
about third century
in the portal I passed
glanced barely at me.

But I saw
he had my face,
the thinker
with consummated glance.

Then my vision reached
that rift beyond
o'er which it is said
none passes and returns,

Glimpse beyond of after life
spellbound faces
celebrating,
bright garmented,

Ancients and moderns,
poets, philosophers
schooled in Athens.
How could I return?

The dream did, to more modern day;
before my group
was to start,
I stopped by the Greek Church.

No longer leaning by the door
I took a seat,
then all were filled,
and the holy assembly's

Procession began,
Was it Christ's
own Saint Nicholas,
Rescuer from perils, joyful?

Beside him flaming
haired woman or man or
Archangel Michael,
and I woke on Christmas morn.

A deeper reality
dreams me,
I have seen his face
face as of the living priest
of the living dios, or All.
Does that living reality
yet burn a miracle
for all who yet stare into its incandescent glow—
World waiting
in us
to heal itself?

Exercise

1. Please remember an especially close friend and/or mentor
who is no longer with you.

2. Enter into meditation, allowing to arise whatever memories
you have of this person. Don't bother to record them during
the meditation. The essential ones can remain with you until
you make your notes afterwards.

3. In the meditation be aware of what feelings come to you
when the specter of death is so near.

4. Make your notes after the meditation, trying to remain in
a poetic, imaginative mood. Ask yourself what death and your
own death mean to you.

five

The Ancient City as Symbol of the Individuation Process

Many people have dreams of, and also fascination about, being in a familiar town which is at the same time unknown. This city of the interior world embodies the image of the self—the possible, "whole being," as total fulfillment of the person in the cosmos.

When in our dreams we are led through the streets of the often ancient places, then we may know our true natures just as the Greeks knew their "polis," the Jews envisioned the restoration of Jerusalem, and other people have been able to represent something holy and complete in the image of the city. That inner image is of the "self."

It takes courage to work on yourself. To work on oneself from a Jungian or process point of view, one submits to the possibility that something exists beyond rationality and beyond what one identifies with. In Western history the rational point of view was necessary to separate us in part from the instincts, but now we have reached a time when we need to reestablish contact with those instincts. Likewise, the development of reason was a necessary phase in the freeing of the intellect from the religious powers which imposed a rule over free thought. Today, again, it may mean that we are free to discover the power of spirit or psyche as an inner manifestation. Likewise, in our personal history, it may have been necessary to identify with a portion of our experience to free ourselves from the unconscious, but then comes a time when we need to reconnect with both the vitality and spirit or psyche within ourselves.

Inner work can lead to a place in oneself beyond the selected parts of oneself with which one usually identifies; that place beyond, is the secondary process. Dreams of the symbol, "the city," may be a vehicle for this journey beyond rationality and one's more narrow consciousness and personal identity. But the ancient city is just one part of a larger framework on inner life and symbolism which we need to understand in order to appreciate this particular image.

Jung wrote about the extensive symbolism of alchemy as a reflection of inner processes. Alchemy, although an ancient and medieval art, mirrors the inner life of modern people and, in fact, alchemical images reappear in the dreams of modern persons. Jung explains this latter point by way of suggesting that a particular inner development of Western people may have stopped during the period of the alchemists; individuals may need to pick up again that development, today. Indeed, the individuation process of modern Jungian psychology may be a way of picking up and continuing this process of inner development. The symbols of the process of individuation that appear in dreams are images of an archetypal nature which depict the centralizing process, or the production of a new center of personality.[1] This is what alchemy is like. It is an attempt to rectify the one-sided nature of ego consciousness and balance it with the underlying nature of the human being as "psyche." The appearance of the symbolism of the ancient city, as one possible symbol, must be seen in that context.

Jung writes about the situation of the alchemist:

> The self wants to be made manifest in the work, and for this reason the OPUS is a process of individuation, of becoming a self. The self is the total, timeless [person] man and as such corresponds to the original, spherical, bisexual being who stands for the mutual integration of conscious and unconscious. [2]

Jung carries out a study of the individuation/centering process. In this particular study, he examines several hundred dreams of a person; the person was not his analysand, and his dreams were submitted to Jung by a colleague. We are told at the beginning of *Psychology and Alchemy*, where this study is reported, that the person is one of excellent scientific education. More recently it has been revealed that the person having the dreams was a world famous physicist. I hesitate to add that note. But I can do so with this clear conviction: given the nature of the objective psyche or collective unconscious, such dreams as this person had, come to many.

Jung selected from among the dreams a workable number on which to make his comments. The development of the dreams over time shows the centering tendency about which Jung has spoken. Jung's comments are a veritable mine of information about the psyche's symbols. Many of this person's dreams were about the anima. Jung defines this archetype as ". . . a personification of the animated psychic atmosphere." [3]

Jung writes in *Psychology and Alchemy* that: "It almost seems as if the differentiation of the intellect that began in the Christian Middle Ages, as a result of scholastic training, had driven the anima to regress to the ancient world." [4]

Referring to the individual dreamer whose dreams are being studied, Jung says, ". . . . the conscious mind with its rationalistic attitude has taken little or no interest in her and therefore made it impossible for the anima to become modernized (or better, Christianized)." [5] If we think of the anima as roughly equivalent to the inner life of a person, man or woman, then it is easy to see that this equality of the human being is depreciated in our time. Jung continues: "By acknowledging the reality of the psyche and making it a co-determining ethical factor in our lives, we offend against the spirit of convention which for centuries has regulated psychic life from outside by means of institutions as well as by reason." [6] Therefore, a person in analysis today can feel a high degree of isolation. Turning again to the person whose dreams he is studying, Jung writes:

This intensified isolation [of the dreamer] can be traced back to vision 21, where the union with the unconscious was realized and accepted as a fact. From the point of view of the conscious mind this is highly irrational; it constitutes a secret which must be anxiously guarded, since the justification for its existence could not be explained to any so-called reasonable person. Anyone who tried to do so would be branded as a lunatic. The discharge of energy into the environment is therefore considerably impeded, the result being a surplus of energy on the side of the unconscious: hence the abnormal increase in the autonomy of the unconscious figures, culminating in aggression and real terror.[7]

I have seen this taking place over and over again with clients doing analytic work. For the individual to take the psyche seriously, to involve it as a factor in everything he or she does, is a big step indeed. Therefore, the above description may fit the experience of many people at one point in their process as they attempt, through a Jungian analysis or through process therapy, to make contact again with the ancient wellsprings of human life.

We want at the moment to deal with only one representation of that process, the ancient city. I say it is one symbol. But symbols have many meanings, and it is by means of seeing how this symbol is connected with others that we may gather something of its broad meaning.

What would represent the psyche, as something greater, more profound than ego consciousness? Certainly, the ancient city would have that quality because it represents something greater and more complete than the single person, and at the same time it represents our roots, the roots of civilization. A little later we shall return to the specific qualities of the ancient city taken from another context in Mumford's *The City and History*. For now we shall look at the connections of this symbol to other symbols: drawing upon alchemy.

Let us return to Jung's statement found at the beginning of *Psychology and Alchemy*. There he writes: "The symbols of the process of individuation are images of an archetypal nature which depict the centralizing process or production of a new center of personality." [8]

The symbolic city is one of those archetypal images which signifies the individuation process, the coming of a new center of the personality. This center is the equivalent of the god-image and the opus, or lapis, as alchemy represents it. Jung reports that similar ideas or forms are found in Gnosticism: "the Anthropos, the Pleroma, the Monad, and the spark of light [Spinther]." He then quotes from the Codex Brucianus: "From Him [the Creator] it is that the Monad came, in the manner of a ship, laden with all good things, and in the manner of a field, filled or planted with every kind of tree, and in the manner of a city filled with all the races of mankind . . . " Jung then continues remarking on the connection of the Monad with the field and with a city. He likens the Monad and the city, to the lotus in Tibetan Buddhist mandalas with the Buddha dwelling there. The holding part, the rose which holds Christ as the paradigm of the self, is also like the Monad and the city, and there what we call God is god manifest in creation and in the human being's inner life.[9]

In another section Jung links, from alchemy, the Monad and the lapis. "The term lapis," he states, "is used all through the literature for the beginning and the goal."[10] In addition "the lapis is . . . a living being . . . a good friend and helper."[11]

In dream life, the symbol of the lapis is the mark of potential inner development. *The ancient city has all these meanings.* I repeat Jung's statement: "The inside of the 'golden flower' is a 'seeding place' where the 'diamond body' is produced. The synonymous term 'the ancestral land' may actually be a hint that this production is a result of integrating ancestral stages."[12] We see by this, the connection of this inner work to the production of a subtle body awareness, such as was described in the previous chapter.

Now in a modern dreamer these things might come together with awareness of being in this body. This indeed happens in the dreamer Jung studies in his series contained in *Psychology and Alchemy.* In the dream concerned, ". . . Four people are going down a river: the dreamer, his father, a certain friend, and the unknown woman." Jung lays emphasis on the fact that of the four figures, three are from the conscious realm. He writes: "The dreamer connected the upper and nether regions . . . he has decided not to live as a bodiless abstract being but to accept the body and the world of instinct, the reality of the problems put by life and love, and to act accordingly." [13] Jung then quotes the Rosarium as saying: ". . . man is generated from the principle of Nature whose vitals are fleshy." [14] Jung pointed out in another place that the four figures pre-figured the temenos or protective container—which also corresponds to the Monad, field, and city.

Returning again to the problem of isolation to which we have already referred, Jung adds: The crash to earth thus leads into the depths of the sea, into the unconscious, and the dreamer reaches the shelter of the TEMENOS as a protection against the splintering of personality caused by his regression to childhood. [15] The ancient city is one symbol of both that safe place for the work of transformation, and the image of the process, itself.

What might this connection be, between the real body and the diamond body? Jung writes: "The spirit (or spirit and soul) is the ternarius or number three which must first be separated from its body and, after the purification of the latter, infused back into it. Evidently, the body is the fourth." [16] To work with one's body in a dreambody way—recognizing a reality which is both physical and psychological—is to open the door to the preparation of the subtle and of the diamond body.

To near the summary of this section, one must recall that the lapis and the self are parallel. There is a further parallel; that is Monogenes who is the offspring of the Creator. This again refers to the mystery of body made manifest in our lives, and our inner lives. As Jung points out this is a heresy—that there is something of the deity in us, in our own bodies. But it also seems to be, and here I am agreeing with Jung as well as stating my own belief, that this god made manifest is the secret of such rituals of transformation as the mass. It means the symbolism behind the mass is universal and its mystery to some people, is efficacious, on an inner and profound level. [17] Jung writes:

> The symbolism of the rites of renewal . . . points . . .
> to man's innate psychic disposition, which is the result
> and depository of an ancestral life right down to the ani-
> mal level . . . The rites are attempts to abolish the sepa-
> ration between the conscious mind and the unconscious,
> the real source of life, and to bring about a reunion of the
> individual with the native soil of his inherited, instinctive

make-up . . . The case before us proves that even if the conscious mind is miles away from the ancient conceptions of the rites of renewal, the unconscious still strives to bring them closer in dreams.[18]

This is why we have Jungian analysis and process work. Arnold Mindell ties the archetypal images of alchemy such as Mercurius, to body symptoms in his statement: "A long personal or cultural history that has repressed the pagan gods encourages illness."[19]

Mindell continues on the subject of the dreambody: "The dreambody is a diamond body . . . "[20] He adds ". . . the dreambody is basically a perception system and that consciousness means awareness of our ability to perceive . . . The dreambody may well incarnate in matter during life and become a dream near death."[21]

Mindell shows at length how to work with the signals of the dreaming body in relation to physical symptoms and relationship problems.[22]

The diamond body, the dream symbol of the ancient city, and the dreambody are parallel formulations. As in Oxyrhynchus sayings of Jesus, "Therefore know yourselves, for you are the city, and the city is the kingdom."[23]

The dream of the ancient city has continued to occur to me. I cite the following example. The motif of the city is here combined with centering as you will see.

Now the dream entailed a journey by bus. I thought to myself as I rode the bus about a return to my origins. It felt wonderful. This bus took me to a part of the city where I had never been before. This seemed like Norwich. It was beautiful. Everything came together in a quaint center. The bricks of the highly styled brick houses were maroon [like my apartment home during childhood]. It had such atmosphere. I wanted to show this to my wife. We passed through what seemed like a partial tunnel, but still in light. And wonderful flower banners were on the walls of the buildings on the right.

I realized as our bus swung out from there that we were going on quite a journey. I saw the towers of Herod during the era of the second temple. There was the whole skyline of this ancient city of Jerusalem. The colors of the many buildings were bright in the clear sunlight and slight haze. The journey seemed now to be circular and, I thought, we are going on the outskirts of this ancient city. Oh, I looked to the right, into a great crevice, and there was the Plaka of Athens. We were heading in that direction. I would be able to see Athens, too. In the first part of the dream when I passed through Norwich, little did I know this journey would take me in such further places of splendor. And I hadn't realized before the dream of this bus trip that Norwich of the dream world contained these other ancient cities.

Exercise

I ask you to reenter an early memory in which you felt connected to the universe, the vast, the Tao energy in things. To others this exercise could seem as a link to other places and times, even previous incarnations. To you it may be a walk in the ancient city or your most special place in the world.

six

The Ancient City—
Amplification of its Historical &
Archeological Meanings

We have seen from Jung's study of the writings of alchemy how full of meaning is the ancient city as symbol. When we reach into such documents of the inner life, then we may become aware of at least part of this meaning. Now in this chapter we turn to certain historical aspects of the ancient city, for the light that may throw on our topic.

In the dark mists of time there was the city. The ancient city in our dreams harkens to us from such a dimly lit space of the past, conveying the city's history, rich in many meanings. What is real outwardly about the ancient city with its long history is true for the psyche, as it takes up this same image in dreams, to express what is as Jung says, beyond our abilities to otherwise express. In a word, we have been this long route ourselves, with its mistakes and losses and its spiritual and psychological triumph. Our individual lives did not begin with our births. Rather, in our dreams are reflected our ancestors' trials and progress.

We come on the scene with something in our souls which has stood humans in good stead over our long course of history. The symbol of the ancient city reflects this process. Lewis Mumford's writings about the ancient city give us indirectly, phenomenology of the psychological factor termed the self. The self was for Jung a controlling center in the psyche/body as a whole representing a more pervasive awareness than that of the ego, the center of consciousness. When we look at the historical qualities of the ancient city, which Mumford describes, we shall see also how they symbolize aspects of the self.

The city starts off in history as a sacred place. In dreams, the ancient city is one of the most sacred spaces. Lewis Mumford writes: "Starting as a sacred spot to which scattered groups returned periodically for ceremonials and rituals, the ancient city was first of all a permanent meeting place."[1]

Mumford shows how this meeting place then developed. Many cities such as Athens began on the natural formation of the citadel; such an outcropping of rock with its immense potential for fortification, was often of major importance in the choice of location. Near at hand to the shrine of the god or goddess found on such a citadel, was the royal palace. The ruler was, as is well known, often considered to be the god's or goddess' representative on earth, although this was not always the case in ancient Greece. Priestly quarters developed in time near the citadel.

Mumford speaks of the citadel as being the city's pilot project, and he says ". . . this accounts for the fact that so many of the characteristics of both city and state today bear the imprint of ancient myths . . . "[2] Formed at a sacred place, the ancient cities were imbued with these deeper layers of culture expressed in the image of deity and the deity's story. These structural elements of myth from ancient times are alive in our concepts of the city, whether or not they are recognized as such.

The king in the ancient city with his quarters on the citadel, could act for the god or goddess and for the community as a whole. The ruler's being, then, became the matrix for the formation of the qualities of the future citizen, as Mumford points out. The king, and indeed the priests, had the power of leisure in which to develop themselves. The king also had the power of private property with which to pursue goals and purposes; he could take risks and make choices. Hence there is in the king of the ancient city, a rudimentary symbol for consciousness.[3] Indeed, in Jungian psychology, the king in myth represents the principle of collective consciousness.

Mumford shows how the privileges of kingship were later transferred to the city and/or the citizen. An example of the latter is immortality, conceived in Egypt as belonging to royalty and later, through *The Egyptian Book of the Dead*, given to human beings as a whole. The city is at first a place of gods and goddesses; later, humans can see themselves as being like gods and goddesses. Therefore, Mumford states, "In the end, the city itself became the chief agent of man's transformation, the organ for the fullest expression of personality."[4] We might call that in modern psychological terms, the basis of the individuation process, which indeed is what the self is.

Mumford lists the extremely important functions of the city as storehouse, accumulator and conservator leading to transformer. It is easy to see the necessity of stores of foodstuffs. Mumford points out that the lists and records of amounts of such discovered in Ur, were part of humans' earliest writing.[5] This form of recording could later be transferred to the things of the mind, emotions and feelings. The ancient city as symbol of the place where writing developed then points to the psyche's uncanny power to reflect upon events and to communicate to and among all its parts. Again this features in the definition of the self, which like its image in the mandala, relates all parts to the other parts and to the whole. In much the same way, awareness works utilizing symbol and language to unite the disparate parts into the whole of individual and collective existence.

Let us now consider the labors of the city. In the village all the tasks of life might have been done by one man and one woman along with their family, and sometimes groups of families. In the city, by contrast, these various myriads of function were performed by specialists. In that sense the city is a conglomeration of specialists. And everything exists in the city. Those who are best at specializing may be most adapted for living in the city.

What is virtually lost today is the person who can do all the things for herself or himself. Zorba the Greek is somewhat the person who can still do everything. He says, "Boss, I can work with my hands," he plays the satori, mines for ore, negotiates with priests, settles disputes, etc.

The city, as an image of the self, then, contains everything—all the specialized parts, the archetypes, the senses, reason, etc. It is complete or whole. The city is as Mumford says, the uniter of past, present and future. And its memory is greater (in volume) than any one individual.[6] As such, the city is a symbol of the collective unconscious.

In all these ways, the city of the dream symbolizes the self, the totality of the psyche. The outward aspects of the ancient city which we have considered are still there for us, to grasp and to understand the self, a manifestation of the psyche's tendency toward wholeness.

With this symbolism in hand perhaps it can become more clear why the image of the sacred ancient city held such a fascination for me and also the woman I described in chapter one. As I read the words of Julian of Norwich, I recall how many times I too have gone to the city she describes, as resting in the heart. For me it exists in the soul. This city is full of awe and excitement as I go there in my dreams, always recalling that I have been before and that it is my favorite place. When I find in the dream that I am in Norwich, then I am full of the greatest excitement and cast about to find the right street where I might reach again the sacred place, where the divine mysteries are performed, incessantly it seems. And this sacred place is in my own dreaming process and soul.

Indeed, the image of the ancient city is close to the healing process. Jung writes about the connection of the image of the historical city with the sacred protected space for psychological work; this includes the kind of inner work or centering described in chapter three. He says: "The drawing of a spellbinding circle . . . has been used since olden times to set a place apart as holy and inviolable; in founding a city, for instance, they first drew the SULCUS PRIM INGENIUS, or original furrow . . ." Jung goes on to speak of his patient, the scientist: ". . . the dreamer [in his modern dream of the circle had] succeeded in establishing a protected TEMENOS, a taboo area where he will be able to meet the unconscious . . ."[7] As I work with new clients, I find over and over again that their concern is whether their work with me will be a safe space in which they can open up to the psyche. The knowledge of the symbols such as the ancient city, is important to us as we allow the great psyche to speak to us in its depth where it resonates with all of history.

This centering process of coming within the sacred, inner space is as Jung asserted, close to the healing process itself. Now we are going to touch upon two more aspects of the self: one is its capacity to form a center of judgment in addition to that of the conscious ego; a second is the presence within the self of opposites of creativity and destructiveness.

The self contains that quality of awareness from some deeper source which is so vitally needed in our dealing with the problems of the modern world. Miguel Serrano shows us how knowledge of this awareness emerges from the work of Jung; I think it comes particularly from his concept of the archetype of the self.

Serrano quotes a letter of Jung to him as stating: "I am guarding my light and my treasure . . . It is most precious not only to me, but above all to the darkness of the Creator, who needs [humans] Man to illumine higher Creation."

Serrano continues:

This thought . . . is illustrated by his story of the chief of the Pueblo Indians, Ochiwiay Brano, who believed he was helping the sun to arise at dawn. Jung had tried to find for modern man a myth as transcendent and vital as that one, and in the end, after years of work, he revealed it in a statement which summarizes all his labors, namely, that man is needed TO ILLUMINATE THE OBSCURITY OF THE CREATOR. In a Jungian sense, the extension of awareness is ". . . of the inner light which emanates from the mysterious 'center' of the person . . . " As the alchemists used to say, "[Human beings] Man must finish the work which Nature has left incomplete."[8]

To me this explains in part why an understanding of alchemy has exerted such a powerful influence over my work with my own dreaming process. If we are needed by nature to reflect her, then as part of nature, we are both nature and reflection. We imbue all life with that possibility of knowing. Then all our experience, if accompanied by awareness, has within it the seeds of light, the alchemists' splithers or divine sparks; these, we have seen, are represented as the garden with the fountain in the center, and the ancient city, etc. Hence, Serrano's statement that it is indeed the self which is, in the Chinese concept of the soul, in its impersonal part, which goes on after death. And it is awareness deriving from the self which can bring a significant and deeper perspective to bear on the problems of modern life. Arnold Mindell's work on this subject is very important in his concepts of deep democracy, city shadows and global processes.[9] I highly recommend the reading to those readers with a bent to applying insights and methods of depth psychology to world problems.

The linking of the symbol of the ancient city, to the "self," has indeed laid the groundwork for further implication. The self contains all the opposites, including the creative and destructive, as does the symbol of the city. There is something about our modern cities which is unmistakably destructive as well as creative. This root is also present in the ancient city. Athens, for example, was destructive toward smaller Greek cities in order to acquire the wealth used in the age of Pericles, for her cultural ascendancy. Today, the urgency of dealing with this destructive aspect of the city is brought home in this statement: "Urban planners and parliamentarians must radically change the face of the worlds' cities or the people in them will not survive, says . . . Arcot Ramachandran, the undersecretary general for the United Nations Center for Human Settlements."[10]

For that change which Ramachandran proposes, a kind of "global awareness" is needed, such as outlined by Mindell. Such awareness has very practical application not only to work with individuals in their healing, but to work with the processes of small and large groups, cities, nations, etc. Discussion of the interrelation of this awareness in both the inner and outer worlds, will comprise the remaining chapters of the book.[11]

It is time for a summary of these chapters to this point.

Posit the *psyche*
its images are old
as old as life itself,
as old as the most ancient city;

be touched by the *ancient images*
whose images give form
to life itself,
bringing its draught to you and to my lips,

so that I may speak to you
of them
and you may hear and feel
the sacred life:

if you but touch and feel the sacred
as it comes in those images of our dreams
then I and you will be *healed;*

the *body and psyche* are one;
healing rests upon this event
when we become "whole," or "healed," cured or not;

this same psyche/body *embodies consciousness,*
whose limits are unknown,

this same psyche/body
is like the *diamond* body
resting on the ancient, extending to the unknown.

seven

The Importance of
Dreams, Myths, & Mercurius

Dreams are a major source for our story. Since ancient times, dreams have been the subject of major studies, for example from Artemidorus of Daldis, who lived during Trajan's reign.

It was in dreams of the ancient Greeks that gods and goddesses made their epiphanies, or appearances, to men and women. As such, dreams have a clear connection to the stories of John, Melanie, Jim, and Michael, which are to follow. I would like to share with you a soliloquy on the meaning of dreams to me:

If I were to tell thee of dreams
stranger still they seem
even than thirty years before
when I first began recording
these watchwords of the night.
And I have done so since;

Oh it seems my whole life
might have its telling in these masterpieces,
the great sea washed up
on my doorstep.
Still my life receives from this sweet source
this stream which pours out
from the island mass
dropping in its deep green waters
the very secrets of life itself,
pouring there into the sea.

I mean if I were to tell you my dreams
I and Heraclitus would tire
the sun with our talking.
Such an individual world he thought
was that of the dreamer
but one which connects one, too
to all that is,
to all peoples and times
to all places and scenes.

All the great philosophers of ancient times commented on this vast subject, the world within, which is at the same time one with the world. Jacob comes to mind. With his wrestling with this inner figure he came to knowledge as few in his time and derived a blessing which kept him afoot with the inner world. Joseph, a diviner of dreams, ascertained the influence of dreams on people's minds all his days. Hippocrates also credited to these events of sleep, a knowledge which could not be gained in other ways and posited that the soul can know causes of illnesses in the images of sleep. Dreams, too, were part of the cure at Epidauros where Aesclepios visited ardent devotees seeking his presence in the night.

Dreams it seems are markers of history: Constantine's dream of the cross was conceived by him as leading to his victory the next day, and he showed his gratitude by showering privilege on the previously persecuted Christians. In modern times, there was John F. Kennedy's dream or image the morning of his demise: he told an aide, a man could go on a high building and shoot down below . . . Not too many moments later, a startling world event occurred.

Tricky can dreams be, too, with ancient Hermes behind them taking pleasure in misfortune as well as the fortuitous. Greeks credited Hermes as mediator of dreams, as with his golden wand he brought sleep. Dreams in ancient times were thought the epiphanies of goddesses and gods.

I am convinced that dreams observed over a period of time lead to a new center of the personality—what Jung called the self. I am sure that dreams on a daily basis are a great guide for the conduct of one's life. Important scientific discoveries have been made through the dream: e.g., Kekulé's formulation of the concept of chemical resonance in the benzene ring based on his dream image of the uroboros—the snake biting its tail. I have seen evidence that dreams may seem to comment on previous existences and also crucial points of psychological development in one's genetic line. There are dreams which seem to exceed the limits of ordinary space and time, connecting us to real events such as the death of a loved one in another place.

Bigger than life figures seem to create us in a new way in some dreams, figures that have an immense impact and importance for the individual. Dreams can be of great help in times of distress. It seems at times that even the dead communicate to us, and that we are aware of their condition through dreams. Dreams fascinate the laymen who may otherwise not be apparently interested in psychology or the imagination. Dreams can be the source of healing.

Process work may have an attitude toward dreams, which is compatible with those of Tibetan Buddhism. A dream is not a fixed reality. It, too, is moving on, evolving. A dream is in process. The process method for working with dreams involves drawing a circle around the portion of the dream which fascinates one most. Then one is urged to work with that in an active way, following the switches amongst the channels of information. One follows an evolving process, using the skills of process meditation (chapter three).

"Man is genius when he is dreaming," states Akira Kurosawa. Van Gogh as portrayed by Kurosawa, in his film *Dreams,* relates these words: ". . . All of nature has its own beauty and when that natural beauty is there, I just love myself in it. And then as if it is in a dream, a scene just paints itself for me . . . it is so difficult to hold it inside."[1]

Myth and Mercurius

Symbol and myth, Jung said, are the best possible ways of expressing something which is otherwise inexpressible. Myth, therefore real, was Jung's conclusion. Myth indicates the reality of the inner world as it suffuses all of life.

Joseph Campbell speaks of myth as a secret place where the cosmos seeps into the individual life.[2]

Arnold Mindell, expounding on the one world theory of Lewis Thomas, the biologist, writes: "Each of us functions in a way which can best be understood by looking at the events of the entire world."[3]

When we use myth in this discussion, we mean myth, legend, fairy tales. Von Franz writes:

> To me the fairy tale is like the sea, and the sagas and myths are the waves upon it; a tale rises to be a myth and sinks down again into being a fairy tale. Here again we come to the same conclusion: fairy tales mirror the more simple but also the more basic structure—the bare skeleton—of the psyche.[4]

Von Franz goes on to say that myths and legends express more of national character and culture as compared to fairy tales which are again more basic to the psyche.

Process work, as well as Jung, speaks of the important thing of living the myth of one's life. For you, what might that myth be?

Where are some of the places you could get hints about your personal myth? Here are some possibilities:

a big dream in the Jungian sense;
a dream with which you began an analysis;
the essence or symbol behind what you thought you
wanted as a child;
that about which you dream the most—again the
symbolic quality of it.

To be able to work with myth is to be able to work with what *comes up* in the body. Process work sees many body symptoms to have a dreamlike quality. Myths help to interpret dreams by giving a picture of the archetype or structure behind a particular happening. Another view of process work toward myth can be understood if we first look at the world as a wholistic organism, an Anthropos, as Arnold Mindell suggests. He goes on to say, "Myth then represents giant conflicts in the global or regional or cultur-al pattern."[5]

Following one's personal myth could, in some cases, be an antidote to disease. Following one's dreams allows one to have some healing impact on oneself using their hints. Learning to tune into feelings in a part of the body confirms the right way to go and can be a point of judgment about situations.

I would like to turn now to a specific figure from Greek mythology, Hermes, also known as Mercurius. He appears in myth and dream.

Mercurius

I have known for some time that there is something missing in the vision of Christianity, as such. I hadn't realized that Mercurius complements Christ as an image. What Jung says, and this is so important to me, is that consciousness arises from the unconscious and unconscious processes. Modern people are bereft of soul, and a religious attitude toward nature, themselves and others. This, coupled with the rootlessness of modern people, pre-vents them from having a connection with the sources of life and the spirit, which have sustained people throughout the centuries. Rationality and morality, while they have been necessary in the development of consciousness, can be stultifying if they are allowed to rule alone, without recourse to a sense of the founda-tions of life and the spirit.

These foundations are dynamic, energetic images which under-lie consciousness; Jung has called them the archetypes. To correct the imbalance created by the denial of spirit occasioned by the principle of reason alone, it is vitally important for people to come once again in touch with the vital patterns of life. In order to com-plete this process one must meet the self. The self is at once the highest and the lowest. In fact, it contains all the opposites: light and dark, masculine and feminine, good and evil, material and spiritual, etc.

Perhaps the self contains what we are currently rejecting. This is why Jungian and process work are so important, both the work in individuals and in groups; they help to reestablish that connection again with secondary processes, other parts than those with which we identify, or our primary processes.

In the West the self has had a certain phenomenology. Into the pagan world exploded Christianity. The emphasis on the light seemed necessary for the evolution of consciousness. And Christianity went all the way in that direction with its emphasis on a totally light quality to the god-image as represented by Christ. As this was not true to nature, there had to be a compensation within the psyche. One of the most important of those manifestations was that of Mercurius, or Hermes. Mercurius had an ancient tradition, and in the middle ages he was taken up as a central image for the phenomenology of the alchemists.

Hermes/Mercurius represented various aspects of the total psychological experience of the human being. Jung writes: "In comparison with the purity and unity of the Christ symbol, Mercurius-lapis is ambiguous, dark, paradoxical, and thoroughly pagan . . . The lapis . . . represents all those things which have been eliminated from the Christian model."[6]

In this same essay, Jung writes in another place of Mercurius ". . . as a *process* that begins with evil and ends with good." Indeed, Mercurius is an image of the process of transformation.

The way toward encountering the self is not necessarily an easy one. In fact, Mercurius also symbolizes that process. It was projected by the alchemists on their work with matter. But their formulations give a perfect picture of an imperfect and at times arduous process. Mercurius combined with a light, conscious side, gives a representation of totality, the self.

The fluid, volatile qualities of Mercurius complete the more rigid, structure of consciousness, and form a new unity with it which restores the original god-image, or self, in the human being, but complete not only with consciousness but that original verve of life!

Mercurius is found in process work. The ailing collective view represented in ancient mythology as the king, is revived by the healing powers of Mercurius who is by nature a unity of opposites, opposing forces. Process work speaks of primary and secondary processes within the individual. In relationships we speak of two parts. They are the same.

I would like to recall for you some of the specific qualities of Hermes/Mercurius.

The Archetype of Hermes

Hermes, you are important to me.
I have met you many times throughout my life,
but I did not know you were the pattern.
First I understand you are the mediator of dreams.
Then I know you, too, under the name of Mercurius,
in your pivotal role in healing.
Principally, I know you as the one of the Way.
Open roads and openness between those who
are journeyers is one of your trademarks.
You move around a lot.
The marriage elopement is one of your
specialties as there people have left the communities
in which they grew up
in order to experience in more depth
the absolute starkness of the marriage partner.
You, too, are found at the piles of rocks
at the passes, known as the Herm; there
the spirit of the Tao is felt
in the image of Lao Tsu, the great master.
There one knows what it is to be in
time, real time.
You, too, are the guardian of the gate.
You preside there where souls go deeper inside
and you are their guide, as psychopomp.
As this already implies death as well
you meet souls and lead them to the island fields.
You are phallic as the masculine
source of life. You are shameless,
even discussing openly your parents
Zeus and Maia's conception of you.

You are like the angels bringing messages
of the gods and goddesses who inspire dreams.
You are known to be wild.
As Phallos you come and go.
You with your golden wand bring sleep
and mediate the world of dreams
You are known as a companion
to men and to women, a god who
keeps company with us, visits us
and partakes in our daily round.

Is Hermes relevant to a religious outlook? Why do so many people think of the source of all beings and things as God? That is a question which has preoccupied me for years. When I was a child, I remember distinctly a moment when I asked myself: If God is the Creator, then who created God?

There is something valid in the tendency of so many people to have a view that God must be behind all things. As a child and young person, I had several experiences of the nature of God. One concerned just this impression of a force behind all that is and all that happens. I remember the first time this dawned upon me. Everything was connected. Everything belonged. The force I felt in my heart, the yielding to something beyond me and the confirmation in other's sharing these experiences with me—all these revolved around a central impression. I thought the universe must truly belong in God's hands, and I felt when I shared this impression with others that they experienced something similar. My job became to be present, if possible to that happening.

Many are the years and many are the trials since that time. And yet I guess you could say that I have been looking for a point of reference since that time. What could explain these early childhood experiences? Why are there throughout many epochs and civilizations, experiences and impressions of just this same phenomenon, of a sense of a wonderful unity with all that exists?

This is where Hermes as an image comes in. Hermes became for me that point of comparison between my intuitions of childhood/youth, the knowledge of the god experience as a transcultural phenomenon on the one hand, and the creator core concept, on the other hand. Karl Kerenyi quotes Walter Otto in this statement about Hermes: "He must once have struck the eye as a brilliant flash out of the depths, that it saw a world in the God, and the God in the whole world."[7]

I truly believe one of the great contributions of Islam is (using Kerenyi's words) to see the world in Allah and Allah in the whole world. I can understand and appreciate this Muslim point of view.

Marie-Louise von Franz points out that alchemical thought was very important in the ancient Islamic world. It remains a source of possible connection for Westerners both with that side of religious thought for Muslims, and for Muslims' connection to Christians and Jews, and vice versa.

The god-image in dream and poem

I would like to report to you below the dream of a modern person I came to know through my practice. It is followed by a poem of his which portrays the dream experience.

> I came into a chapel. I took a seat at the back. Then I saw a figure appear outside though the front window. He was taller than life and statuesque like the god figure of El Greco in *The Coronation of the Virgin*. He was in white robes [as that figure is], and his outer garment, the cloak, was black and shiny, of modern material. Presently he was inside and sitting at a central desk. On the table at the back of the room was a book[s] of common prayer. There were only some little books marked prayer and one marked Prayer and Yoga. I went to the figure in the middle of this one room. He recalled seeing me in Georgia [Russian Orthodox?]. I was part of his group [place of religious transformation]. He handed me a beautiful copy of the *Book of Common Prayer*. It was red with gold trim and letters. He had not seemed to object to the chair I had occupied, an old-fashioned dowel-backed chair which creaked but was very welcoming. His hair was white-grey and rolled

down to his head in rivulets. The liturgy moved to the inner sanctum, ahead. It was an intimate fellowship. People, very young people, were standing around the walls. I was definitely very young like a student or scholar.

Could Jung be right, that the deep level of the unconscious at times represented itself in persons in conflict? He had in mind the level of the archetype of the self, that archetype having a life of its own and being active in the creation of human history. Terrible outer events are sometimes a reflection of inner images and powers (Jung's seeing, for example, the destruction within Germany before World War II as an expression of an archaic, native spirit, Wotan, an archetype).

But Jung had spoken in *Answer to Job*, of a drama initiated in ancient Israel, reflected in Christian history early and late, of a god-image (archetype), namely, that of the self trying to realize itself in men and women.[9] Jung had said further that this god-image wanted to incarnate in many people. It could, if their compassion for all the parts of themselves was great. Perhaps those same people by the increase of awareness, sought something akin to god-likeness for, Jung said, people wished to become as gods, just as in the depths of the psyche, the god-image wished to realize itself in human life.

To get back to the dream I just described: It was a dream of the god-image portrayed like a man but bigger than life. That godlike inner figure had visited our modern dreamer in the emanation of one who in heart was pure as the driven snow and who was in his more outward garments black, in a modern sense. The dreamer could see that the archetypal drama described in Jung's *Answer to Job*—taking place in the figures of Enoch, and John, author of the apocalyptic Revelations—was indeed, related to the drama of his own inner life, as it had been to Jung, the alchemists and others.

That drama of the god-image, that of the archetype of the self, took place in our dreamer. *The White and Dark God*, which he thought of entitling his dream, was indeed as his own experience, an epiphany of this sacred power. It was a drama which could take place in any person. The white and dark god was a reconciling symbol, uniting opposites, and as such, a milestone along the way of the individuation process, where all parts get included.

My client thought it fortuitous that his plans to be a minister had not worked out. Instead, the drama of the divine child had been enacted in him, the inner drama of God's realization within individual men and women, in the reconciling symbol uniting opposites. The path of the ministry, it seems, would have been FOR HIM a path in one direction, namely toward the white god, where the unification of opposites—goal of individuation and of the alchemists— might not have been possible for him.

Perhaps this person's dream, like that of the alchemists and more accessible than Jung's, could show what may be trying to happen in the inner depths of modern people; it may yet be, in a small way, an answer to the drama of conflict within the collective unconscious which if not worked out in individual lives, may yet trouble our continents and world.

The dreamer's poem:

Christ my thanks to you for light
resurrecting in sleep an image, lost
I thought, of god who visits the soul in night
an ancient patron of inner path, host
for citadel quiet centered prayerful hear
magnificent desk, magnanimous gaze release
The Book of the Common Prayer and there to start
within scarlet, gelded covered singing leaves
the true place, true beginning more
the way I always was and now to feel
the youth, hallmark of self restore
this my place in unbroken circle seal
    I always knew God as image kind
    now I knew he replenished mind.

The importance of the Mercurius material to me is that it helps me also understand my own mystical experiences when I was a young person. For example, I remember a poem which a friend shared with me. In the poem the person stated that he would rather stand by the door than go into the furthest deeps of the unspeakable mysteries, himself. He wanted to stand by the door to help others to enter. Of course, this is similar to the Bodhisattva vow, in which the enlightened person reenters life experience, so that eventually all beings may be enlightened.

The parallel of my youthful experience to Hermes' role of being at the gate, or door, was the one which struck me. True, Hermes, in contrast to my mortal position, is a god, an archetypal power beyond all human measure. It could be dangerous to identify with a god. But to be inspired, as I was, by an understanding of my experience was not dangerous. Moreover, the connecting of one spiritual experience with that of a different tradition i.e., alchemy, gave a tremendous credence to the inner life. Inner experience was everywhere and in all times (as Jung pointed out) the same, or at least similar in the important motifs. Rather than detracting from my religious belief or experience, the discovery of parallels to other traditions added to my experience.

My friend William Kennedy was fond of saying that we are evolving toward a culture in which I can be right and you can be right.[10] This is the perspective I offer to you as I discuss my friends' and clients' encounters with Judaism, Christianity and Islam in the next chapter. May their story be a hologram of how the world parts, currently estranged, could come together.

Bringing Together the Parts

It was the conviction of the alchemists and writers like Goethe that the god-image contained both the light and dark. Obviously, that was true of Mercurius. The dream material I have cited shows how these opposites in the god-image have appeared in a modern person.

How is it possible to portray more of the meaning and reality of that to modern people? On an existential level, we can see that a person who tries to be *too good* often brings harm; a person who is angry, but who is inhibited by ideals from expressing his or her needs, may pollute the atmosphere around him or her, with negative vibes. Likewise, countries which behave as if they were superior culturally to other countries, sow the seeds of animosity and distrust.

As Jung was brave to show, the god-the-father aspect of the Christian god-image did not always behave in the most idealistic way and was balanced or compensated by the image of Christ as all-good, completely light. For human beings to identify with a completely light god-image could bring about suffering and destruction in the world. The analytical psychologist attempts to have few illusions about all this. One cure for such an inflation of regarding oneself as nearly perfect is the recognition, through dreams and inner work, that the god-image is both light and dark. That inner image of wholeness which the Jungians call the self, contains all the opposites: light and dark, good and evil.

What can all this have to do with rapprochement on a world level? As Jung had indicated, if the German people of the 1930's and 1940's had been able to contact and integrate their inner image of the teutonic deity, Wotan, their own problematic god-image, they would probably not have become possessed of its negative side, wrecking havoc on the Jewish people and other people. Today our task seems to be to offer people the experience of finding the light and dark sides of their god-images.

This can be done in inner work and in groups. As Mindell shows in *The Year I,* opposites such as light and dark are part of every field whether that field is an individual, a group, a nation or a world. When people of different and opposing nations and cultures can experience this psychologically, the tendency toward evil can be integrated. This takes away its great power to harm, because it is destructive when either we identify with it as a part or we identify another group or culture with evil. The various parts are a part of every field, such as my psyche, my nation.

A field, in the sense of physics, is like an underlying pattern, a matrix which can later be actualized. Jung likens his conception of an archetype, for example, to the pattern of the crystal which we see in its actualization.

Groups and cultures express such patterns. It is a well-known experience of groups, for example, that if one person strongly emphasizes rationality, another person will be drawn to, or *dreamed up*, to express its opposite: feeling. One part compensates for the other, bringing in the total picture, so to speak. If you interview the person who has spoken out for feeling, you may find that he felt drawn to go beyond his own personal position, because of the one-sided position taken by the spokesperson for rationality. We, as process workers, understand this as parts of a field coming into play to express the total field. The person drawn into speaking for emotion is somewhat used by the field, dreamed up.[11] We, as process people, like to break up that identification of any one person or group, with any part. And we are able to do this by showing that the parts are not really personal, but expressions of a field. After that, what is indeed personal may be more easily expressed.

When the personal identifications with the parts can be relieved, the parts can become fluid, so to speak. At any one time, one might be the spokesperson for rationality, or feeling, for example. When that shift takes place, it is possible to get down to real discussion and problem-solving. The invisible image of opposites, such as high and low, can thus be relieved of their unconscious grip over group processes. Let us invite opposing cultural groups to the table for such an experience. Before we proceed into the next section, I would like to tie together aspects of our theme, in these points:

1. The individual, and the images of the city and the cosmos, are connected;

2. When the individual dreams of the city, he or she is potentially being connected to the image of the self, and perhaps the cosmos;

3. The cosmos may reach us as individuals through the image of the city as image of the self;

4. Our realization as individuals may involve the evolving of the image of the self both as inner and outer;

5. This is what John, Melanie, Jim and Michael have tried to do as reported in the sections to follow.

John Dreams a Big Dream Awake

John told me his dream, his face deeply moved by his experience. I could only credit myself as being another post along the shore of a vast ocean, a post like himself, each beckoning to a more vast self and yet each stationed in mud and fastened to the floor below.

He told me, "I saw myself as the communion body and blood. These figures appeared before me, and I realized it was my body and soul." I had never heard anything like this. The latest sequel of John's stories was more intense; his inner life seemed very intense at all times. All along there had been a parallel between the happenings of his life and the deepest mysteries of the Christian experience.

I wondered how many people there are like him, people with soundings into the spirit which resemble what is collectively worshipped in Western culture. Were some people held back in speaking of their experiences, perhaps feeling the experiences were too strange? Perhaps for some, the way of understanding such experiences was limited by either a view which regarded the world as completely spiritual on the one hand, or completely physical on the other hand.

My giving account of John's story was for these people, and for myself. John told me more of the dream. He said, "I remember the loaf which was rectangular and small and was the bearer of twelve small nipples. The eucharistic wine was also there. They were me. There was no difference between me and them."

What could all this mean, I wondered? The appearance in ordinary space-time of a central mystery of the Western tradition, was staggering; moreover, that this profound reality presented itself paradoxically as being also like the mundane, was even more striking. And twelve small nipples on the communion loaf were a detail not to be overlooked. John said they reminded him of Diana of Ephesus. He said he had seen a picture of this figure in an art history book. There, more than any place in the ancient Western world, was the image of the feeding of the devotee by the goddess of the many breasts. I just suggested to John that he allow his imagination to feed on this image (to feed on him in your hearts, as the Christian liturgy suggests). His imagination was jarred. There one of the most beautiful of the feminine images, that of the breast, is presented to the devotee as a religious experience. The whole body is touched. Indeed, as we discussed this image, John told me that all the pores of his body and mind opened. He was the vacuous liquid, the permeable substance, receptacle of the Spirit.

If I am going to go all the way in my interpretation of this most expressive of images, I must return to what John brought up next. He brought up the connection to the Grail.

I went back to Chretien de Troyes' *Perceval or the Story of the Grail,* the first written version of the very old tale. John, as I looked at him, was, I realized, not so unlike Perceval. John, with his big hands, his native intelligence and wit, gave the impression of one, rough hewed in the social graces, but stunningly persevering in what really matters in life; he was like Perceval, at once missing the point through reluctance, and yet continuing on the quest. Once, for example, John had spoken of his kinship with the outwardly plain looking and poetic Abraham Lincoln, who in Stephen Vincent Benet's poem had characterized himself with the line, ". . . oh Lord, I am that old deaf hunting dog, and I will go on when the others have given up the scent . . ." Like Perceval, John had a sense that had missed his timely moment in which to realize himself. In retrospect, I could be glad for him for the sense of loss and lack of realization which he had carried throughout his life. These gave John the deep longing for true realization for which the Grail stands as one important symbol.

I immediately turned to the passage where after years of desolate wandering, it seems Perceval will again have a chance to discover the repartee to that most enigmatic of questions: "Whom does the Grail serve?" This was when he was in the hall of the mysterious Grail castle for a second time.

John and I just talked. I said you can't believe what a moment that was in Perceval's life. Here he had left his mother and set out on the route to become a knight. That venture was richly rewarded. He met a knight who could teach him, Gornemant of Gohort, just as his mother had admonished him that he would need such instruction and intuited that it would come his way. The reward was great because he came unto the very court of Arthur. What a moment in history, or was it history infused with myth, the deeper history, so to speak. Not only did he arrive at Arthur's court, but even with his clumsy beginnings, he was made a knight of the round table. This would be more than enough for most people. But for Perceval that very naive quality of his life led him into an encounter with what is of the greatest value.

John and I came back to that point where Perceval was in the Grail castle for the second time. I asked, what is the most valuable thing. That is the Grail. What is the thing above all things? That is the Grail. What is it, that which sustains? What is the food beyond all food? What is it that people hunger for, you and I, John? John answered that from his own experience, only one thing really sustained the body. He said he meant sustained past all illness and fear. He then spoke of a dream. In the dream he said he had visited the garden of a dying friend. However, in the dream there was no indication that this man, who had been diagnosed as having pancreatic cancer, was indeed ailing in any way. The dream showed that in the garden was a round pool. The pool sustained the paradisiacal garden and the man. If he was going to die, it was his picture of what it would be like for him after death.

John and I said together, referring to the pool in the garden, ". . . that was like the Grail." Likewise, John continued, when I learn something deep and incontrovertible about my body, that, too, is like the Grail. I asked him if he had something in mind. Yes, he said. He was thinking about a very recent experience. I noted his anxiety and fear. He went on to relate that in a recent period in which he had taken some time off to walk at a retreat center, he had made a new discovery. When he had time to walk and to be quiet, then something happened to his body which was so profound that he was no longer afraid so much of the time. He pointed to the spiritual practices that he completed at the retreat center as also part of the healing of the body which had taken place for him there.

This led now into one of the deepest aspects of the Grail. If it was all that we had said it was, that which could enable a person to go beyond sickness, fear and death, then that would help to explain the mystery afforded it. That is, if we could appreciate from our own experience that what is of the spirit is able to transform human need and suffering, then we would be on to a clue for understanding the Grail and what was behind the Grail, what the Grail represented, so to speak.

I asked John to go into his own interior world for a minute and find out why he had made the connection between his dream of the eucharist and the Grail. He said that if he were to talk about his own life, the only way he could explain it would be to acknowledge that it was like a bowl, a bowl or Grail in which he had asked at crucial moments for light, or awareness, to understand his task. He said he was glad to be able to say such things to me, because he felt that others might misunderstand him and think he simply prayed out of the admonition to do so. He said there was always a critic in the background who judged such statements, but that it was important sometimes to let the inner spirit speak. That spirit *knew*. His bowl was like a container for offering his thoughts and experiences to the illumination of the deepest motivations and indeed the deepest forces behind life, and then those forces could fill the bowl, so to speak.

That spiritual and psychological awareness sustained his efforts, gave him food for his journey, brought out a part of him which transcended his daily concerns. At the same time, it made those daily concerns and everything he did meaningful. When he was buoyed up by the images behind this lifetime, images which had come to him in his dreams and experiences about his own true nature, then these fed him and sustained him as he attempted to carry out the tasks of this lifetime in the world. So, he said that for him, that was the meaning of the cryptic question: ". . . whom does the Grail serve?" I suggested that we read from Chretien's own account of the high moment in Perceval's life, and we went to the passage where Perceval's hermit uncle tells him:

The man they serve is my own brother,
my sister, and his, was your mother;
and also the rich Fisherman
is that king's son, son of the man
who has himself served with the Grail.
Now do not let the thought prevail
that from the Grail he takes food like
a salmon, lamprey, or a pike,
because from it the king obtains
one mass wafer, and it sustains
his life, borne in the Grail they bring . . . [12]

Now John and I just sat. The muse worked the Grail legend into our hearts. John was, in one respect, the bread and wine of the host. What he would do with himself in this lifetime might be an encouragement for other people. Others might draw sustenance from him, simply from what they perceived of him. In their interactions with him, a few people experienced the grace of their own lives. This was John's gift. I invite you the reader to consider with me some of the modern ways people have become in touch with the spirit of life, one the Romans called Mercurius, that same Hermes of ancient Greece. Balance is needed for all things beautiful and Hermes had such a balance, uniting male and female, and darkness and light. By Hermes, I mean that alive moment when one is in no division and when one's labors, whether they be love, gentleness, scientific theory or poetry, flow from one's inner source.

As Arnold Mindell has so artfully pointed out, people in the modern world need all the parts. A contribution which each of us can make is to find as many of those parts as possible in oneself. As the ancient poet Rumi has said: "Never hear one party without the other. Till both parties come into the presence, the truth is never made plain to the judge." [13]

Process work would call this the perspective of the two parts which is the foundation of relationship work as well as work on one's own soul and the world. Dreams are a major source for contacting other parts of the great self.

eight

Intuitions of Connections to
Other Times as a Modern Process

In one's dreams, imagination and even one's experience, one may feel connected in an intuitive way to other times or epochs. It is important to consider some light which Jung's discussion of the anima can throw upon the subject.

The Historical Anima

Writing of the anima, Jung says: "She likes to appear in historic dress, with a predilection for Greece and Egypt."[1] "The anima of a man has a strongly historical character," says Jung.

Jung continues his description of this aspect of the anima or soul:

> As a personification of the unconscious she goes back into prehistory, and embodies the contents of the past. She provides the individual with those elements that he ought to know about his prehistory. To the individual, the anima is all life that has been in the past and is still alive in him.[2]

Speaking of the possibility of going to Rome as a young man, Jung writes that he felt he ". . . was not really up to the impression the city would have upon [him]."[3] He elaborates on the sensitivity he felt to ages past and the many concrete representations of the lives of people of past civilizations which he would have encountered in visiting the ancient city of Rome.

Jung's reactions make more understandable the very strong impact which my first visit to Athens had upon me. Combining the ideas of the historical quality of the anima with the dimension of the city as representing the self, one can see the force and power

which a visitation to Athens or Rome might have upon one. That
visitation could come in real life or be felt in one's dreams.

I trust as you the reader follow my account of these episodes
of Jim, Melanie and Michael, that the importance of the historical quality of the anima will become clear. I believe this is what
gives us some of our ideas and dreams with which we are connected with times past.

I also had such an experience in 1975 which I shall share with
you in the attached poem.

Memory Quintessence

The fourteenth century reliquary
silent, many-sided, cone copped
remnants within of God knows what
lavished in the stone of its day
and intended forever.

Surrounded by protective grove
of magical, knotted and ancient
trees
intricate leaves,
giving home
to flying souls, their weighty weightlessness,
grounded in these.

December dusk has laid you
Medieval city
where the twilight of years
the haze of timelessness
and I—on this its third day—
can be turned, returned
to some event three December centuries past
in this very churchyard—
allotted a new me now
can I ever guess what?
Across the way my bus is pulling
to its stop.

Norwich
Norfolk
1975

Jim and Melanie

Jim, a therapist and supervisee, came around to the subject again which he had touched upon a few times in his work. It was about the goal of his life. To Jim at this time, it seemed a subject he could actually approach.

It had an arisen quite innocently. Jim was doing some process work with his friend, Melanie. They had been doing a project together, and some differences had arisen. They were trying to work on these differences.

There were two other people present when Jim and Melanie were talking. Jim said he decided to go beyond his hesitation and say to Melanie that he felt when they did workshops together, that he "carried her." He said that by this he meant that when they did work together, he might have to work with something which had come up for her within the group session, or during the break when the workshop leaders met. At first Jim said that Melanie expressed strong dislike for the idea he had raised. Then, in the way of process-oriented psychology, she began to let the at-first rejected idea happen in some way, in order to see what might emerge into awareness.

Jim said that Melanie said something about wanting to find out what being carried was like. She came over to Jim who was lying sprawled out on the floor, and Melanie simply took a position in his arms like a bird might perch upon a bough, or a baby rest in a mother's arms.

Jim said that the changing of this argument from a verbal level to one in which bodies expressed themselves by the positions they took put him in an altered state of consciousness. Remembering back he said that with her taking such a vulnerable and open position in order to find out more about something, his feeling was deeply touched. He remarked that his strong but seldom spoken awareness of her as a Jewish person, came to the fore. He said it was as if he could then speak the thoughts which were often beneath the surface. But then he had an actual vision. He saw himself as living in the fourth century when things had actually gone badly between Christians and Jews. He realized that he had a connection to those times as in another incarnation. I realized that this is the way the anima in her historical quality might feel to a modern person, what I was discussing at the very beginning of this chapter. And he said he realized that his discovery of that was at the same time a recognition that his own life must contribute in some tiny way to the unraveling of the twisted, strife-ridden strands of communication between Christians and Jews which had emanated from those times.

Another big event came for Jim. He said he knew that the time had really come in his life to try and work more directly toward his goal in life. He was looking for ways to explore this. He was considering things he could do. Always, in the example of the Buddhists and the Dalai Lama, he asked what was his motivation. He knew he would soon have an opportunity to speak out on a larger level.

Then he had the following dream. He said he was walking up a hill in his favorite town in Europe. He said:

> I went on the path above the ancient building. I knew the path was an ancient one. I loved the dirt and the feeling. I noticed that there was a house just over the hill.

I myself was getting excited as Jim described these events. He continued:

> I looked down into a well of stairs, and people were coming out of the house and emerging up the stairs. The house was an ancient one and did face out on the other side of the knoll, but here, it was built into the earth. The people who emerged were Jewish, and the man who first appeared, was beautiful. He had dark hair and dark eyes; he was thin and strong.

Without a moment's pause, Jim then said that he took the dream as an immediate encouragement to open a way to heal in some way the ancient split of Christians and Jews. This was at the time when, forty-four years after the end of World War II, the countries of central Europe were emerging again as distinct entities. Jim said with a brush of his hand that it was as if the souls of the Jewish people killed in the holocaust and war were again emerging into the life of the world.

It so happened that I had been thinking about these two ancient world religions at that time. I was aware of some of the historical connections between the two groups, and I asked Jim if he would be interested in finding out more of the story. He said he would. We agreed and met for coffee later in the week.

I was excited when I met with Jim. I had a story. I was piecing together the strands of history. I felt I had a comparative discipline in my Jungian world to compare modern people's experience of psyche, with knowledge of myth. I, standing with currents of two powerful sources, had at that point no knowledge of how the two could come together. It was yet to emerge how these ancient religions and the modern course of the individuation process could spring into a meaningful "third," a live manifestation which united them in the case of Jim.

Jim and I chose as our meeting place our favorite Greek restaurant. We enjoyed the hot coffee, with its tangy aroma and bitter and sweet taste which reminded us both of Europe and the Middle East.

I asked Jim, can you imagine what a time that was in the first few centuries of what we call A.D., anno domini, a Christian phrase implying that group's perspective on the events of the period and following. I was determined to try and avoid some of the prejudices with which this whole period, and the following centuries, were rife.

I told Jim that as far as I knew I had ancient origins myself in the early Christian world. I told him that my name Roomy was originally spelled "Roumi" and meant Christian, Greek or Roman living in an Arab context. I was already feeling a little defensive, so I tried to bring out my feelings to Jim. I said that if I were to bring out some of my findings and views to some Christians, I feared rebuff, rejection. With some Christian people, I said I felt that I had to toe the line, to be "orthodox" in order to be listened to.

At that moment I became aware of an uncomfortable way I was sitting. I was going out of my way to prove a point; I was already defensive around SOME Christians, imaginary Christians in my mind, who might not be open to my interest in Jews. I had digressed, I acknowledged to Jim. I felt such an affinity for Jewish people in a way, which at that moment, I could not explain. I just said that I felt a deep connection with them. And, I said, that in my thirties I had wanted to find out all I could about World War II and the incursions made against the Jewish people at that time.

Where were we? I asked. Oh, yes, I added quickly, that I wanted to report what I had found out from some historical sources, about the first centuries of this era. It was as if Jews and Christians were twin sisters in a very confusing and somewhat disturbed environment of the first through fourth centuries. The empire-minded Romans of that period had reason to oppose both groups. Some Romans held a view of their gods as being angry and in need of propitiation in order to avoid the natural catastrophes which might be the work of the gods. Those gods again demanded the slaying of animals and the eating of the meat and sprinkling of the blood on various objects.

Christians and Jews were opposed to these measures to an extent that led to martyrdom in the first instance, and rebellion and death in the second. The Romans saw the refusal of the two groups as a threat to the safety of the community, as the gods could be easily angered at failure to adhere fully to the rites of protection. The refusal of Christians and Jews to conform, each from their own spiritual foundations, was tantamount to treason in the eyes of Rome.

Not only were Christians and Jews persecuted but they persecuted one another.[4] Each seemed to violate something the other considered so basic, so fundamental to their aspirations and very being as peoples. Some members of the opposing group thought that worthy of out-and-out persecution. I was about to go further with this point when Michael, one of Jim's Jewish friends, walked in the restaurant. We invited Michael to share a glass of wine with us. We told him that we had been discussing our hope for more rapprochement between Christians and Jews. I said that at the very moment he had walked in, I was just starting to think of the "two parts."

I continued, "Let's say there is a part in each person with which he or she identifies." I asked Jim and Michael if they wanted to play my game and explore this further from the point of view of process-oriented psychology. They said they would, but that they might not be typical of other Jews and Christians, as each group had members within it who were somewhat suspicious of the mythological approach of a Jungian type of psychology, such as process work. Each was quick to point out that both religions were quick to see themselves as peoples of revelation. In both Jews' and Christians' minds, revelations were central in their perceptions of themselves and their peoples. This separated them somewhat from Greeks, and from modern people who might emphasize the power of myth as underlying particular religious formulations of particular peoples. I said that in our discussion I would take on that controversial part as it could also be a possible point of unification between the Jewish and Christian views.

Each of my friends objected. If they were going to take on the parts with which they could identify, then they weren't going to have any "psychologizing" of their religious views, submitting special, unique events of revelation to comparisons with other peoples in far parts of the world. They were referring to the Jungian view which posits a substratum in the psyche out of which all ideas and perceptions of meaning arose. That concept, they felt, belittled them, they said.

I said that brought up the Greek part, Greek in the Hellenistic sense, not so much the Romiosyne sense, which had developed during centuries of interaction with the Turks. This part, I said, does not want to belittle anyone. Just look at the Greek world in the early centuries of this era, I continued. Every nook and cranny of the inhabited world had a shrine to this god or that goddess. No diety was left out.

"That's just the point," interjected Michael. "The Lord our God is one God."

"Yes," said Jim, "and if I take on my part fully, I will say that this divinity is also three in nature." Jim then smiled and said, "It is hard for me to take on that part because as far as my Christian sense of devotion is concerned, I also have a place for Mary as the fourth part of a quaternio, with God the Father, God the Son, and the Holy Spirit." He added that the Holy Spirit may have been regarded by certain early Christian theologians as being of a feminine nature. "Also," he continued, "I have been affected deeply by some of the other world religions such as Buddhism, and certain of their practices are part of my daily practice."

The atmosphere at the table was becoming open. I saw twinkles in the eyes of both my friends.

"Whenever people identify with a position as ultimate truth," I continued, "they are experiencing something like the 'logos' was for some people in the early centuries in the West. For those people, it is principle above every principle. People will die for it, and sometimes peoples will kill other peoples, so supreme is that principle in their minds."

Jim noted that Jung had written about that subject. He said that Jung stated that the West had made rationality and morality into absolutes in order to free themselves from instinct and the pull of the unconscious. Those had been necessary phases in the development of the Western mind, for example, in the freeing of reason to pursue scientific endeavor. But the individual had been left bereft by this development, for he had lost touch with those very realities, celebrated in myth and ritual, which had sustained human life and meaning for centuries. How to get back there . . . of course, without losing what we had gained through the centuries of development, Jim added.

Michael seemed interested and asked Jim to say more. Jim spoke of how by following his own dreams, and working over the material of these nightly processes, he had become aware of another kind of development taking place in him, pertaining to the development of the inner person. That had been his experience, he said. It was as if some of the principal miracles and events of the Christian tradition had been working themselves out in his life; he said HE was the material being changed like the persons and events described in the scriptures. So, he added, that when I asked him to play the part of identifying with the Christian view, he was unable to do so.

Michael said he was relieved. He said it meant that he and Jim could really talk. He said he had known all along that Jim was more fluid in his views but it helped him to hear it said again.

This awareness that one is not completely identified with any one position, I said to my friends, is the basis of process work with groups and couples in conflict, as well as the individual. One starts with what a person identifies with. That part, what we call the primary process, must first be supported genuinely when working with a group or a person. As that position is heightened, an interesting thing takes place. Something else starts to happen. A person will start waving his or her arms, looking away, etc. We call that a double signal. Something else, a process not as close to awareness, a secondary process, has started to happen.

As both Jim and Michael had tried to be identified with their primary processes, I had noticed something else taking place. What interested me in Jim was that his backbone would move forward at about the level of his waist. I asked him if he would allow me to work with this. He said he would. I asked him to repeat his statement while moving forward at this one section of his back.

"Strain, strain," he said he felt. I asked him to feel it more, at which point he sat back in his chair and breathed a deep breath. He said he wouldn't try to do any more than he was already doing. I noticed that his back now remained in a stable, relaxed position. The figure who had been pushing him from behind was changing. I was glad for Jim. I recalled something that Arnold Mindell had said about heart attacks. He pointed to a figure in some cases, pushing from the back in a different time, out of sync with the heart. I mentioned this to Jim, and he sighed deeply again. Then he mentioned a dream: he had dreamed that morning that a student had told him that his class was quickly filling and that if Jim did not want it to be larger than ten people, he should let the registrar know there was a cutoff point for class registration.

Something was completing itself in Jim. It meant his registering this fact and not allowing a situation to continue in which he would take on more students and more work.

91

Just then the sun began shining strongly through the clouds outside the restaurant. Jim said the "not-doing" would give him time to go on with the inner development prefigured in his dream. He said to him, the number ten symbolized some sort of completeness with what was already at hand. If he could just be with that, there was no need to do more.

I reflected to Jim and Michael that not-doing was more like the meditative quality of some Eastern religions and the contemplative side of Christianity. It was like being in the desert, the heritage of the religions emerging from the Middle East. Jim, by attending to his inner process, was perhaps doing all he needed to do for now, in his interest to help reconcile Jewish and Christian elements. He agreed with me. He said that when he was in retreat recently he had turned his attention to a problematic relationship, and he was surprised how the whole dither he had been in, changed inside him, and he saw his unity with this person in a powerful light. When he had seen her again in real life, he said he felt that both he and this other person had somehow gone beyond the unimaginative, oversensitiveness which their relationship had reached.

Michael said it would be a long time before many Jews trusted Christians again but that he trusted Jim as he followed his parts, which often seemed in opposition to each other. Perhaps Michael added, "It was as the scriptures of Judaism had said, 'I have called you into the Desert' . . . " He was referring to the stillness involved in Jewish mysticism.

I thought then, well, we could be tolerant of quiet and active moments because they are a reflection of our very "self" in the Jungian sense of our totality. Accepting oneself in any moment whatever it was like, would be tantamount to acceptance of the self.

Now Jim leaned down further on his knees with his hands so that they were resting just above his knees. His back leaned forward. He took a deep sigh. Then he mentioned that there was a little sense of pain and weakness in his lower back. He put his hand back there. Then he began moving in his chair. He asked if I would tell the story about the Mexican guy to Michael.

I said when I was twenty I met a young Mexican guy. The guy's small hands were very expressive like an artist's. He liked to talk on a deep, feeling level, his eyes enlarging and his face turning and lifting like those paintings of medieval saints. He and I were involved in the student groups in the church. Then I recounted what happened one Sunday. I saw Nazarro go forward at the end of the church service when the minister invited people to join that church or transfer their memberships there. Nazarro made his way forward down the long aisles to the front where the minister was standing. He asked Nazarro: "Do you accept Jesus Christ as your personal savior?"

Nazarro paused as if hearing the question for the first time ever. Then he looked up gently into the minister's tense face and said, "No." Then Jim said to Michael, "You know, I have been carrying that story in my memory for the last few weeks. What it must mean is that I am called on by the example of Christ and the Great Spirits, to live my life as fully as he and they admonish."[5] He said, "That takes me to a point of freedom, as far as religion is concerned. That is the crucial point with which to start."

Jim said he was picturing the fields of Ontario. He was outside his town, opposite it across some fields, and studying winter as it expressed itself. The sky was grey with moving clouds, and the old maples reached again and again away from the direction of the wind. He was lonely. He said only now as he recalled the scene did he know what his emotions were then. He was lonely for like-minded people who hunger after truth, inner truth like that among his closest friends in Toronto, as they had tried to appropriate in their lives the new methods and perspectives of Jung. For Jim, Jung had had so much to say about religion as an inner process. That really appealed to him. Walking on that Ontario lane, he thought, I could help bring Jung's perspective to people. The drama of the scriptures and the mystery of the mass and complicated interrelation of the figures of the godhead—these were experiences of the inner person, the soul. This, he thought, was what he should bring into the church.

Alas, no one he could find was interested. The various churches on the whole, perhaps with the exception of the Quakers, had other perspectives. Jim looked up. He said, "You know, that was one of Jung's goals, to understand the relation of the trinity and quaternity, and the problem of evil. I don't need to do what Jung tried to do."

Jim said he was enjoying this process; it was helping him to think. Just then he scratched off a small, old dried scab on his knuckle. I asked him where he had gone, seeing that his attention had turned inside. He looked embarrassed. He said he had seen just an ordinary diner made out of chrome metal, like the Greek families have on Long Island, New York. I asked him to keep looking. He said he saw himself having a good time there, having a piece of pie in the company of his lively wife. A tear rolled out of the corner of his eye. He said it was the realization that the ordinary moment is the great gift offered to us as human beings.

There was nowhere he had to run to, no group to join, no dream to make literal in life, nothing to do. So much for the grand story of my life, he said with a smile. He added, "'Tis a gift to be simple, tis a gift to be free," as the Shaker song goes, "'tis a gift to turn out where you want to be."

Jim wrote in his journal this note which I include:

In a year such as this
I, true happiness seek
what the change, the difference
just to seek my plain being.

Jim and Melanie: Startling Possibilities

And so the saga continues. Jim told Melanie the dream he had had. He related to me that when he told her, he realized that the dream was perhaps about more than his personal life. The dream had concerned a visit of his to Europe. And in the dream he had come over the hill to see a group of people emerging from an underground part of a building, this part being like a bunker. These people were led by one very special, very beautiful man, thin, intelligent, courageous. Four or five people stood behind this leader. The people were Jewish.

Jim said he ventured a possible meaning to the dream. It had occurred just after the event in Eastern Europe, in which the many countries there were declaring a kind of new sovereignty, as parts breaking off from the Russian empire. So many Jewish people from these countries had lost their lives just before and at the time of the Second World War. Jim said he told Melanie, that perhaps, just perhaps, the souls represented by these people in the dream were again returning. Many interpretations were possible.

Jim told me that when he told the dream to Melanie, he saw her face change from its usual soft, bright and pleasing quality, to one with wrinkles and bumps. The eyes changed from being flashing, positive to deep opaque green-blue which seemed to reach an unending depth. Speaking of the thin, intelligent, figure appearing in Jim's dream, Melanie had said, "Perhaps it is the coming of the Messiah."

The life of dreams was moving on in the lives of my friends. Melanie's dream was a great dream. It was a dream of a whole people and a dream for the whole world. It signified a profound hope for the whole of mankind, a kind of maturing of the species into its full potential. The other great leaders and founders of the world religions had all pointed to a simple, yet far-reaching hope that people could be guided by the divine-feeling spirit within, so that their actions would be in harmony with others and with all of life. The Messiah was not just for Israel nor just for the Jews. This hope which has burned bright in people's hearts for around three thousand years, is for an end of suffering for all peoples. In many ways it is comparable to Buddhist aspirations. I could relate to that from my experience of meditation.

I myself have many aspirations: they range from the desire to provide for myself materially, to profound hopes for all peoples. Still, meditation, like Jungian analysis and process work, provides valid ways for moving toward those aspirations.

I will speak of only one form of meditation here. It follows a teaching by a Tibetan Buddhist Lama, a friend of Thomas Merton who received Merton during his trip through Asia. In this meditation, one focuses in the middle of one's chest, on different elements which form the basis of the mind. One makes a visual image of each of these qualities in turn. As the focus is directed toward the mind, for example, one pictures a white disc about the width of four fingers. One attempts to hold this image. As the successive distractions arise and fall, one attempts to keep this image. Gently the mind is calmed (the true basis of all meaningful action). With each successive consideration of the elements or bases of the mind or whole being, the meditator uses another shape and another color. As the meditation on these foci concludes, the person may find that his/her mind is at rest. The person could gain the special experience that all action based on compulsion is not necessary.

I shared this with Jim. I saw it again as a way of softening the urgency he felt toward helping to bridge the rift between Christians and Jews. Jim was already there. He compared my experience in meditation, and others which he had had, to Melanie's image of the Messiah. Jim said to me that what I had experienced was similar to the experience of the Messiah.

I realized that my comparison of the Messiah with a moment of non-compulsive *being*, which could be conceived on a global basis, was only one small glimmer of this process, called Messiah. The very next day, Jim brought another dream which was to take us all further into our understanding.

Jim recounted this dream. He said: "I was with a Jewish musician. He looked very expressive in his face, like it was completely pure and could express all ideas and emotions. It was as if his face were only a tender, transparent skin revealing a profound inner range of feeling. He was familiar to me like a person I knew, and yet I cannot recall such a person."

As soon as Jim had finished narrating his dream, he exclaimed, "Oh, it is the Jewish savior who came out of the ground!" Of course, he was pointing to the thin, leader figure of his earlier dream.

Jim and I were both in awe. I asked Jim if he could describe the figure a little more. He said, "Oh, he is very beautiful. He had that quality of a man who could lead a whole country. Such a resplendent outer beauty I felt was just like his inner quality, a quality that many would want to follow." I think such a figure could be another image of the self.

In Jim's dreams of the morning, there was mention of movement. I noticed his putting his hands together and taking them apart slightly, so I asked him to amplify his movement. Soon he was moving in a graceful way around my office. His movements began like Tai Chi, very soft in nature. Then his hands came together in the dance. Then I knew he was visualizing, and he started talking about what he was seeing. He said there was something before his eyes, white, and giving off a golden light, like the image of one of the Tibetan deities. Then he said it felt as if some limitations were falling away. He spoke of his friends, those with whom he had discussed his hopes for aiding the process of again connecting Jewish and Christian peoples. He said he knew his friends would be able to help. Then he drew aside a second and added, almost in a whisper under his breath, that the Muslims could come into this, too.

This little piece of work was complete. Jim had experienced something in all the information channels of process work. In the time which followed in the session, he filled out in more detail what he meant by what he had felt, what he had heard, his intuitions of relationships and large processes.

Jim was perhaps experiencing what Jung had called the god-image. That image is comprised of the total possibilities and realization of the human individual. It is the highest intensity of all qualities. It contains all the opposites, the high and low, the left and right, inner and outer, microcosm and macrocosm, the light and the dark. At the same time this image represents the path of individuation and the goal.

All this seemed to fit from Jim's experience. It seemed to be his path to work with others, his friends and students, and some of the members of the world religions, to heal what had been an original unity, that of the twin sisters, the anima Christianity and the anima, or soul, Judaism. That he was continuing to follow his own path of individuation, seemed to be confirmed by the dream. The Jewish leader figure as an inner image was evolving, becoming a real part of Jim's inner life, inviting him to share in music—that movement, sound and sometimes visual aspect of the otherwise ineffable.

A Poem Uniting Two Cultures

For me, Sinai is one of those sacred places in the world which unites two cultures. This poem is a meditation on that sacred place.

Sinai

In your holy temple,
where Justinian fourteen long
centuries ago builded thy sanctuary,
crevice of Sinai,
where Moses had rested,
near at hand thy fire—
fierce love which does not consume,
in just such a place
I, in the centre of the nave
cold and colorful marble beneath
my feet, candelabras, gold
festooned, resplendent light, above,
am afforded rest, here,
centuries have never died,
taste of martyrs' fervor
devotion of icon painters
eyes portrayed inviting eternity,
in just such a place
where I strolled in no hurry
feeling the cool inside
from climate of sunny fury,
I have the morning
maybe my life
the moments golden, dripping
and fed of never ending source,
in just such a place
with great stone flanks,
smooth white interior,
I gaze beyond the iconostasis
where white light falls to the floor,
am invited to share

the mysteries of transcendent love,
in just such a place
where the embodied crucifix
hangs in the center nave
emblem of what can't be explained,
all the guilt dripping away
a reconciled moment between us
and our truest form,
in just such a place
like the Greek churches
of Athens and Nafplion and beyond,
where I've known my true centre
haven't needed anything else
most attracted to God,
in just such a place
the dream placed me.

Muslims at the World Table

From one of the sources of Islamic wisdom, *The Tales of the Thousand and One Nights,* we may draw some unusual insights. Like many fairy tales this collection of stories points to conditions in which the archetypal powers of the psyche may be balanced.

There are several reasons why I would like to bring in a few stories of this collection into our discussion. The first is that the Islamic world is largely unknown and misunderstood by much of the Western world. This first quality is connected with Jim's motivation for helping in rapprochement between cultural groups. He told me this story. He was meeting with a Hebraic leader, a wise old man and scholar from the synagogue. The old leader said in the early days the Jewish leaders could have invited Peter and Andrew and the disciples to sit at table with them. This spirit of inclusion from the beginning could have changed the course of relations between Christians and Jews; the contrasting exclusion, which in fact took place, was practiced in extreme forms in later centuries, especially by Christians and with detriment to all.

Secondly, there is today a need for the Islamic peoples to be more at the world table.

There is another important reason for utilizing the wisdom of *The Tales* . . . It is their intrinsic worth as stories representing the dynamics of the psyche. As Jung pointed out, the less conscious part of the psyche plays a role in relation to more conscious views; this role Jung characterized as being one of complementarity. *The Tales*—according to the translator Dawood—represent the more secular side of Islamic culture. As good fairy tales, they complement more rational, collective views held in many cultures. All these points about *The Tales* are related. The part that has been excluded is the part which is needed for wholeness. Islam is needed by the world, the secular is needed by the sacred, the imaginative story of the inner world is needed by collective outer points of view.

In writing this material on Arab sources, I had the encouragement of Jung. Jung admired Islamic culture in the value this culture gives to eros, or relatedness. I had a firsthand experience of this quality of people from the Middle East when I taught and counselled at a college in England. I found these young people to have a very sweet nature; I liked them very much. Jung's father, a pastor, also had a scholarly interest in Arab culture. Finally, I had an important dream in the late seventies in which Jung encouraged me to follow this interest in writing about *The Tales*.

I turn now to the story of the great woman Scheherazade, or as *The Tales* refer to her, Shahrazad. Her story is the background for all the tales and for their telling. You may recall that the powerful king Shahriyar was enraged. In fact, both he and his brother Shahzaman shared this pervasive feeling. Something had happened to each of them to shock their inner feeling.

Shahzaman first witnessed his wife's infidelity; this led him to his brother's house, where he had discovered what he regarded as an even greater malaise than his own there. Curiously, this realization led immediately to the lifting of his depression.

But Shahzaman, who first had hoped to keep secret his own problem, eventually told his brother both of the discovery of his wife in the arms of a slave, and of King Shahriyar's wife in the company of her ten females and ten slaves. Subsequently, Shahriyar took on the depression.

Both men decided to leave their roles as kings temporarily and to steal into the world to get an impression of how others were faring, in order to have some comparison. It was in these circumstances that they met the great Jinni in the form of a very large black cloud. This powerful figure kept his consort in a chest, but even so she managed to seduce them as well as another ninety-eight men whom she had made love to right under her sleeping husband's nose. Both men were comforted, as they said: "If such a thing could happen to mighty Jinni, then our own misfortune is light, indeed."

King Shahriyar, like his brother before him, returned to his castle and, armed with some insane impulse, slew his wife, as his brother had done before him. Thereafter, according to the story, he took a new wife each night and slew her the next day, thus attempting to defend himself from further personal shame by any wife who might be unfaithful. But his treacherous measures only made his people groan under his despotic and psychotic behavior.

Such a great offense, to the feminine and to human life. Where could help come from? Only from another woman, as it was in the King's lack of a real connection to the feminine that his depression and his murderous malady arose.

What would this woman do for him?

Many of us will recall that the woman Scheherazade devised a plan for the restoration of the King and for the kingdom. She would become the King's wife. In the gathering of people about the King during the evening, Scheherazade would tell the King a story. Then immediately after this story was concluded, Dunyazad, Scheherazade's sister, would say: "How sweet is thy story, O sister mine, and how enjoyable and delectable." Then Scheherazade would say: "And where is this compared with that I would relate to you on the coming night if the King suffer me to survive?" [6]

Such beauty and wisdom were in the stories and the telling that this plan of Scheherazade worked not only on the first criti-

cal night, but each successive night, for a thousand and one
nights. The greatest mystery of the tales is that they are really
dreams. The King wishes to sleep and can't. In this vulnerability
of insomnia in which he must admit his troubled unconscious and
conscience, relief comes. Ostensibly, it is in the form of stories.
As stories, the reader can first accept them and participate fanci-
fully in them. But the stories are in another respect, the King's
own dreams. These he is given in place of his sleeplessness and
anxiety. Scheherazade gives him dreams—and sleep—which heal
him and bring him back to a restored condition. On the life side,
she gives him three sons and companionship for all of his days.

The story always moves me when I hear it or tell it. It is about
an inner transformation, one of the most profound which can
come to a man. It is about feeling, and as a tale, it works on feeling, eros, relatedness.

Von Franz writes: "The anima is personification of . . . vague
feelings and moods, prophetic hunches, receptiveness to the irrational capacity for personal love, feeling for nature, and—last but
not least—his relation to the unconscious." [7]

Scheherazade's tales, like the threads of continuous creative
elements emerging from the unconscious in dreams and fantasies,
offer the possibility of change and renewal. This is the value of
inner work in the individual. As Jung, von Franz, and many of us
have experienced, it is in the recording of dreams over a period of
time and working on them, that the true healing effect of psyche
can be felt. This leads to a new center of the personality, known as
the self. [8] That self then speaks in the realization of the life dream
or personal myth of the individual, such as Jim.

The creative impact of the psyche can also be observed in personal relationships as conflicts, anger and resentments are worked
through. These inevitably involve the discovery of more of one's
own, personal myth and vital energy for living that myth.

As Jung points out, the doctrine of the assumption of the
Virgin Mary, accepted in twentieth century Catholic doctrine, represents at the same time the completion of an alchemical,

Hermetical process of the three, or of the trinity, becoming four. The eros quality of Islam may serve to balance the more logos quality of Christianity and perhaps of Judaism as well.

This poem was inspired by the writings of Nikos Kazantzakis, of Crete, where Arab and Christian influences mixed.

Cretan Beauty

The delicate body of the anima
walks within the lattice of the garden.
The Turkish chieftain has brought her
to his powerful Cretan palace.
She is not a lady of this place.
Circassian, she roamed on horse
in expanses outside her village
where a man was with a woman
when he wanted, and a woman
with a man, the same.
I drink to you, Turkish
princess afield in Crete.
Your chieftan knowing our weakness
has barricaded you from sight
and rightly so, yet some
can look upon pure beauty
and turn the sight to poem
and to them and to you
I gently open the lattice
to bring the sublime to view.

A person's soul or anima may be the inspiratrice. It means contrasting the attraction one might have to the beauty of another person and recognizing that as one's own soul. That is the beginning of creativity and a necessary step to its realization.

The creative always involves contact with what is not so known. The anima is one inner figure which may help to mediate contact with the unformed chaos of the inner world or an outer situation. It was Dr. Rosemary Gordon[9] who first suggested to me the idea of turning the attraction the eyes might have for an outer woman, into a poem.

I add to these points about inner work and the anima this possibility: two people processing things in their relationships[10] can be useful to their respective cultures and the world.

I, too, see the world as many other philosophers have since ancient times, as a living whole. My own immortality partakes of that, for I belong to the whole. My dust particles and chemical elements partake of the building blocks of the universe. My culture belongs to the Chinese, the Arabs, the Greeks, the English, etc. The part I have played in people's lives, lives on after me. Culture never dies, but rather evolves from the portions that each of us allow to accrue to its golden, festooned borders, like barnacles on old wharfs.

Ours is an ancient race, *Homo sapiens*—race not used in the strict sense of the anthropologists. Our race as a world of women and men, resides permanently in the images which arise spontaneously in every culture, time of history and place. These are the archetypes of the un-conscious as Jung has described them. One such concept arising from an archetype is, as Joseph Campbell has pointed out, the belief that in some form life goes on after death.

Jim's myth was to bring healing, that is a perspective of wholeness, to world parts estranged from each other, especially the peoples associated with those cultures arising from the fertile Middle East, and the modern people who are linked to those ideas, either closely or from afar by participating in the modern cultures influenced by those ideas. Many people of good will, will have motivations similar to Jim. There remains the discovery of the means to bring estranged parts in touch with each other. Perhaps process-oriented psychology is one such means.

As the ancient poet Rumi said, it is not possible to know the truth in a dispute till both parties are present. The dynamic system of process work can work with those opposing forces once they are in proximity to each other. Those methods of conflict resolution are part of our repertoire as psychotherapists.[11] Perhaps those in power, which to some extent is all of us, will see ways to become reconciled to all our parts, so that the world may truly become the whole culture that it is.

I have seen this reconciliation take place over and over again at various levels: within the individual, with people in relationship, between parents and offspring, in small work teams, in small groups and large groups. In our collective experience as process workers, our form of conflict resolution has been tried in some of the trouble spots of the world.

Among you as readers, some will want to help heal the world parts. Perhaps that is so deep in your souls it may feel like part of your personal myth. But how to help. Meditate on your personal myth. As Arnold Mindell says, if you take up your personal myth you will naturally occupy your part in the world field or whole.

Conclusion

I hear from others that they go to special places in their dreams. Visiting these places in the night fills them, and me, with awe. Such journeys bring, within their trail, healing.

This should not be surprising; in most spiritual and cultural traditions, special importance is given to the journey to a sacred spot. Perhaps it is where a saint lived and was centered, such as the round stone on which Columba lived on the Isle of Iona, or Sinai, Mecca or Benares. Perhaps it is the place of the Buddha's enlightenment. All such places call up an extraordinary feeling in the pilgrim. Likewise, the inner sacred place also has about it the feeling of awe and transcendence.

Taking, as we have, the mental journey of this book, we have passed through, by means of imagination, a sacred dream place which I knew and built by the seaside and which impacted another person who saw it—one whose psyche was bruised in childhood. It was analogous to the healing process in Epidauros, in ancient Greece, where the god of healing, Asklepios, was enshrined. At this shrine the priest/healer would sometimes have a dream in which there was a synchronicity to the situation of his "client." When that synchronicity occurred, the client was often healed. In my experience with the client described at the first of the book, I see that my dream, and representation of it in the sand, connected with an inner transformation in her.

In the story of the nun, we witnessed how even intractable pain can be impacted when the dreaming, imaginative part of the psyche/body, or dreaming body, is sufficiently allowed to unfold as a process and express itself. Always associated with healing is the centering process, as Jung has suggested. Here our themes converge. For, as we saw in the study of alchemy and Tibetan

Buddhism, the centering process is represented in the psyche's imagination variously as the ancient city and the "self" as contained within the four city or temple gates of the mandala. To journey to the center is the equivalent to finding in one's dreams such symbols as the ancient city; inner journeys to sacred places ARE healing.

That very self at the heart of the mandala represented as Buddha or Christ is brought out in Taoism as a centering practice, the revolving of the inner light, which leads to a knowledge of the "immortal" quality, the timelessness and incorruptibility of the self. This self may go beyond our lifetimes as its representation repeats itself in other individuals born after us. Those individuals may experience this living dynamo of self creation as it works its way out in their lives. They, too, may experience the unity of physical and psychological processes, the dreaming or subtle body, an experience which in itself may be the beginning of healing.

Our study of the symbol of the city took us into its historical elements, through Mumford's studies. This helped us see that outward, objective descriptions of the ancient city's historical process are reflected in parallel meanings of this symbol on an inner, subjective level.

The latter part of our study takes us into the lives of four characters. Here psychology not only touches on historical and individual problems, but also inspires action in the service of cultural and world problems. One of the characters, Jim, experiences how the psyche has a historical quality to it. What seems like an intuition which connects him to ancient places and times is really a manifestation of the historical anima. The anima reflects the animation of the unconscious, and links one to its collective layers, formed out of the collective experience of humankind. And this very material, from the origins of different cultures, may serve as a point in which they can again meet in the diversity of modern life. The nerve of the modern world is raw as cultural units break up and unite. Yet we are formed of a common thread. The touching relationships of Jim, Melanie and Michael may serve to point a way to where the psyches of diverse nations and peoples, and the

seeming splits which have evolved, can again find their ancient
city, their center which exists in all cultures, and which may be
their common healing.

World religions represent collective wisdom;
they are like a library of the human spirit condensed into an essence;
this collective wisdom was built up over generations;
it bears a likeness to fairy tale and myth;
yet those who identify themselves with such religions are
reluctant to see their own faiths as myth;
perhaps for that to ever happen, the adherents to various
faiths would need a deeper appreciation of myth.

Jung's point is that religions are mythologies exercising the
function of reuniting us with our roots;
these roots, the collective experience of thousands of former
generations, are contained in our psyches, as patterns;
Jung called the capacity to reproduce these patterns in each
newborn human, the archetypes of the objective psyche.

When archetypes are again experienced and mark a part of
psychological awareness, the effects are salutary;
the modern individual languishing in the aridity of positivist
philosophy and scientism is again connected to the
wonder of the soul, posited by the great philosopher
Socrates.
As Jung said, he never met a client for whom religion had
not led to his or her neurosis and for whom a rediscovery
of religious attitude had not led to a cure;
What is a religious attitude?
It is one of deep respect and awe for the spontaneous
happenings of the psyche, as the fulfillment or
individuation of a person unfolds;
in the healing center of Epidauros in Greece for example,
once a person had been healed, should that person revert
from awe to a rationistic attitude toward his or her
healing, then a regression would ensue.

Should it be so hard to have a religious attitude?
How does it arise? It arises from experience of the psyche's
depths and its power to guide and heal one.

To live with a connection to one's roots is to be in a place
of oasis.
To live with a religious attitude is to receive and
acknowledge gratefully the water from the depths,
the life-giving water.

What are the fruits of such a life?
They are: wisdom and compassion or love.
Wisdom is the active deciphering and following of psyche's
patterns through life, individual and collective.
And love?
The world is so short on love.
I see a man, a Greek cook, on his walk;
I see a man estranged from his roots,
having experienced so little of love, away from his
homeland.
Love has the power of light, to lighten the soul.

Many of us were brought into deep psychological work
through the experience ourselves, of such extraordinary
love.

Such love coupled with wisdom and skilled,
psychologically informed action, has the power to transform
the world.

This was conveyed graphically, pictorially and in outer form to
the pilgrim visiting the ancient healing center of Epidauros.
Making his or her way into the sacred precinct, the pilgrim would
first see on the right, the temple of Aphrodite, without whom
there could be no cure. The great Sufi poet Rumi knew about this
dimension. Only when his love for Shams had blasted him out of
his post as "religious teacher," could he experience the reality of

ecstasy and poetic wisdom. May it be so for all of us who set upon the journey to the sacred.

The Grail and
a Modern Dreamer's Quest

Some years ago I had lost Norwich as a favorite place to live, replete with a close association with English landscape, comely nature, as well as English age-old culture. These had been my bread. I had imbibed them daily for five years, and they had fed my soul. I had been "at home." This same period had seen my children growing in a whole environment. All that was lost when my job there came to an end, and it seemed we had to move. It was fully lost two years after that, when we returned from another part of England to the North American continent. But the unconscious and soul provide. I was given a union with the mysteries and awe of the Norwich setting. My "Jerusalem," the sacred city, was rediscovered as an inner reality. In the place of the bliss of living in a favorite spot which had been lost, came the bliss of the mystical union with the divine image within my psyche.

I could understand this idea after having read the following interpretation by Ean and Dieke Begg. They write that the historical movement associated with the Grail began at the same time as the fall of Jerusalem from among the possessions of Christendom. They write: "Once the Holy City was gone it had to be reinvented as a mystical god . . ."[1]

The Grail legend and motif are a feature of my interior chapel, the dream setting which has reoccurred with awe and a feeling of the numinous. The feminine in Christianity is also conveyed in my dream's underground chapel with its cave-like border containing the prehistoric bones. Caves in archaeology and inner symbolism are associated with the earth mother, healing, Asklepios, the physician's snake, etc. In the dream which followed in the night after writing this, a crystal on my journey turned into an enclosed bowl, both objects having flecks of gold through their opaque substances.

The chapel of my dreams is after all an "other" world, where people do things differently; it is a realm of psyche. Making the connection between one's dream motifs and those of ancient wisdom is one pathway to the discovery of one's true nature as psyche, or of "the reality of the psyche," as Jung puts it.

My experience was like being found, when it dawned upon me that my Norwich chapel was the Grail. Likewise, the Grail is a Norwich chapel in one of its variations as a living symbol. This was like coming out of the wilderness for me. It had been a long sojourn, in my trying to piece together what my dream of entering the chapel might mean. I had traveled and thought and meditated and read. This book itself was such an effort to understand and share my understanding in its awesome or awe-filling dimensions with you, the reader. Now it seemed to lay more fully before me, the meaning.

Throughout the Middle Ages and perhaps earlier, the Grail had struck people as a living and partly inscrutable motif which was capable of putting the imagination into active hunger for the sublime. Now my dream life picked up that passion, fed my own soul and tantalized me to go on searching. Before the insight of the Grail-chapel parallel, I only had my own experience to go on, though with a parallel to alchemy, it is true. But that parallel hadn't been felt so strongly as it has now that my psyche and my work were connected to one of the Western world's supreme symbols of the goal of life. Knowing that, feeling that, now with the Grail's legend, was like being discovered, and realizing that my path was one which had captivated thousands, maybe millions like me. As the authors Emma Jung and Marie-Louise von Franz write: ". . . it (the Grail) possesses an inherent psychic life of its own which will not allow itself to be confined to any one specific pattern."[2] Emma Jung puts the Grail quest in this historical context. She writes:

. . . Numerous spiritual movements . . . which in part run contrary to the Christian outlook . . . heathen . . . come to the surface in the age of the second fish of this sign. To these movements belong certain rituals of the Templars, the sexual libertinism of some of the neo-Manichean sects [etc.]. On the other hand, there were also movements, such as alchemy or certain Holy Ghost movements within the Church, which were endeavoring to RECONCILE the problem of the opposites of Christ and Antichrist. To these also belong much that is in the Grail poems, for which reason the latter in part appear to reactivate heathen elements to some extent, though . . . they appear to be striving towards a further development of the Christian symbol.[3]

And, Emma Jung continues, the Grail poems had met a further psychic need, to carry forward the tackling of certain problems such as shadow, sexuality and the unconscious. Emma Jung brings in further connections with the symbolism we have already considered in alchemy. She says:

The vessel . . . is often also called a matrix or uterus . . . Mercurius is 'our true hidden vessel and also the Philosophical Garden in which our sun rises and ascends' . . . so the vessel also becomes a uterus for the spiritual renewal or rebirth of the individual.[4]

We have already seen in alchemy the parallel between the walled garden and the interior city. Emma Jung equates the Grail castle and one's supreme goal and true vocation. My dream of the chapel reflects my individuation process: to know and make known the sacred.

Perceval's life task is laid out by our Swiss analysts, Emma Jung and Marie-Louise von Franz. They write: ". . . He is faced with the problem of discovering the form in which the essential psychic life of the figure of Christ continues to exist and what it means."[5] C. G. Jung spoke of Christ as a symbol of the self.

I guess that tells it, in still another dimension for me. I always hoped to be in dialog with those who would reinterpret and help to rekindle the mysteries, so people would have more access to them again. I need to fully make the discovery myself. This reading of *The Grail Legend* is a very big part of my understanding, together with following my dreams. (My interest in the sacred also extends to other religions.) I see that the Grail story comprises my life. It includes my beginnings, as a youth in Christianity. It includes my young adult crises when that world view was shaken for me; in content this is much like the end of the first millennium of Christianity. Like that epoch's crisis, my own resulted in a regression to a more pagan inner attitude, for example, but with conflict, and a sense of loss of religion. This original oneness of myself can only be restored today as I see that my Christian side is part and *belongs with* the fuller expression of the Self, for example, in the Anthropos; such a development is made possible in me through my Jungian studies and analysis, and means including the soulful qualities of myself which are outside the notion of perfection. It no longer has to be either/or for me: I can have my debt to Christian culture and realize it is not complete. I can go my Jungian route toward individual wholeness, with the secret of my own existence, and see myself as partially influenced by Christian symbols and culture. This is the paradox, and it makes me happy to know myself in this way.

I would say that the Kingdom's restoration, which the hero's asking of the Grail question accomplishes, is not just that of the Britons or Celts, or Israel, but of the original human personality in the individual, a return to that person's original nature, being. Jung has called this an apocatastasis, a restoration. That truly is what, I believe, the Grail is about.

My Norwich chapel, in the alchemical sense, is for me, the Grail, "The well-guarded, precious secret of the individual." [6] *May you be opened to your Grail, in whatever form it may meet you.*

A further manifestation of the Grail symbolism can be found in a person's great care about the world. This was the dimension that Perceval in the Grail legend didn't incorporate in his Middle Ages choice to be a hermit, once he had completed the quest. In our age, in ourselves, if these great opposites of spiritual introversion and world involvement could be brought together, perhaps we all, our individual selves and our crumbling ecosystem and stained social fabric, could be healed. This union of opposites is possible. Jung's life was such an example. Perhaps this further development of Western symbolism can be true of people, as two millennia come to an end.

I feel encouraged to go on with this pursuit of the Grail. The Grail can be understood in part as the individuation process, but it is more. It is the goal of a life, and contains the secrets of life itself.

What does it mean to be healed? It may not be such an unreachable and grand notion. When we take account of the opposites in us, and know we have different sides, high and low, spiritual and material, dreamlike and practical, animal and celestial, then we may be in the place between, where a spontaneous symbol may appear, uniting in us, the opposites. Then it is not only a question of whom does the Grail serve, but how we, from this majestic source, may serve.

Poems

Cambridge

An afternoon when raindrops dot my page
and we sit about on Cambridge lawns,
not needing anything other than to gauge
the river's level of peace at St. John's,
For the River Cam though old is new
and newly makes our minds free from care,
ours the watching beneath the willows' view,
ourselves with all watchfulness find repair,
Solitude is such a blessed state.
Yet even its very bliss can be improved,
when your head on my shoulder rests its weight,
and round the shadows the muse is here beloved.
   Fond memories like those are a lifetime worth
   When we can be together in this life on earth.

The Couple
(from an image at Ely)

Love turned its form
as a design intricate—
simple, lively Romanesque tapestry in stone
their love was.

He shared the life
which walked so lightly
impressed in her step
where no heaviness stalked
so subtle the spirit in her chest
he wondered for her,
for the only other like her
was eighty when like that,
needed she a refuge for this spirit?

In the morning he was to leave
on still another sojourn
the couple shared their dreams
Hers about him, his
about their meeting up again,
Love turned its form
as a design intricate
Romanesque leafy, light in stone
caressing vines, leaves curling outward
drinking in sun
in the caring, meeting
turning stone to life.

Highland Lilt

It's incredible, the peace I feel
knowing the suffering of the day
the countless hours rocking with fears
the ought, the shouldn't, and the may.
I glass over that now
for music has held me sway
guided the torn ship of mind
into this quiet bay,
It was bonnie lass, and lilt
and Highland pipes that play
that wooed me to the brightening night
which gently over us lay,
Clear as a bell she sang
pure—as shepherdess, aye
singing over the clearest of lochs
as if the world's first day.

Inverness
Scotland
1974

The Bird Beneath the Stream

Here where the sun turns the heather grass tan
here where nature breeds herself
in the timeliness of conquered thought
time is a morsel for the gods,
passion, as the sea's surface
stretches, azure and sunbright,
a mirror image unwavering,
toward an infinite meeting with sky.

I run my fingers through the grass of words
and pull out the prickle of sadness
delight upon weeds which have their place
where no eye of man has them in its slant,
I have seen a little pink flower
grinning on a stem no bigger
than a fledgling's wing bone
and heard a wren warble
from beneath the thickened mat
where a stream runs singing to the sea.

The West Coast of Scotland
1974

Setting off from Iona

Past Mull
Hidden in mists
a ferry churn and we turn
to face from where we've come:
a link of mountains unbroken reigns
and beyond a still higher range,
how fray our ship was
how small the inn
frailty gains us.
A round stone floor was Columba's bed
bare timber and skins covering his head
he pondered these cliffs
and fiercer even Picts
and wondered if the rocks
would fall upon him and hide him from
the Love of God.
But the message knit
in prayer
the message of why he was there
and slowly the weakness drained into the rock
He left all in the lap of infinity
to shapen within this island fortress beyond
the comely yoke, Christianity.

The Isle of Iona
Scotland
1974

It Takes Dialogue to Make a Poem

I turn my steps homeward
and homeward go I gladly,
This little journey, ah well
you see it has cured me,
I've never been gone for long
the heart didn't yearn for Cyndy,
Being up here in Scotland—
well, it wasn't the same
as when she was wi' me.

A Black Box In Cambridge

In Cambridge gardens' peaceful summer sun,
A forceful image presses on my mind—
those ancient steps to lapping water run
and there a tiny trunk of black I find.
Oh why appear its form as though for me?
I know! Tis mine to publish what I have—
in this attempt within the hidden to see,
in England's noble language vouchsafe.
In St. John's majestic evensong,
the choir spinning sound from Byrd's own pen,
I undergo the ecstasy for which I long
who sing in wonder of virgin, love of men.
  In the sacred garden's now surprising hue
  beneath the stained Rose, a Gardener in view.

At Rye, In Kent

The English village perched on higher hill
than sea seeking landscape turning tan,
of deeper tone its steps, and nobler will
its pointed heights inspired of awe in man,
In highest reach of all, the church's arch
bending the Norman vault to Gothic and then
leading the wandering pilgrim's eye to search
for fainter glimmerings still, of soul within;
for one, it came through clearest window panes,
memories, visited again of sunny light
pouring on village churches, greens and lanes,
his places of many English births—in sight!
   Nature's glistening seascape held it all
   The expanse of soul and beside, the ancient wall.

Passion Repossessed

Back in my mind to Norwich Cathedral
one cold, dark English night
furrows of fog about,
epitome of death, yet
in those chilly spaces, down many a row
the chirpiest greetings, an unyielding glow,

Turning now another eve,
workshop participants bidden adieu,
I settle down for a rest I think,
but mine the wine press of thought,
it will not do,
to forbid the screw another turn or two.

Clever well I ought to be
yet the emotions hang about
I might as well yield,
the familiar animals wish in,
others, having had THEIR flight
(of fantasy) unobstructed by me,
Mine own now need to roust
and in this dark interior chapel
find their rest safe in the night
protected in hay's steamy glow.

Am I closer to others than I thought?
I sit down to tea
with myself,
Eliot please join in
You've known the East Anglia churches,
and now I introduce
a wild, new brand of group—
sharing stories and mysteries of healing,
and in its trail—numen.

England in my Garden

I found England in my backyard
the mossy tips round ancient sites
immense gardens storing visual delights
sanctified buildings glowing—even the bard!
I found historical pathways to famous places
nooks and crannies where fav'rite visionaries slept
castles and stones time's stories kept,
I walked in England and felt her sacred spaces.
No more do I depend on outer forms
England an inner world is for me,
Of all bounds of happiness, the limitless moves,
and marks set by thoughts are passed, and harms
put in place, inner spirit by Thee,
Solitude more than England, my soul behooves.

The White Knight and the Green Knight

I carried you down the Slingun
searched for you on the borders of Kost
wept by the weary Cyril
marched with might mercenaries
down edges of Ebb plain
sacked Goths
and stabbed visiers
the Caliph had maintained
Low, I searched where the Brandywine
twined with the Ebb
and flowed toxic past Malibu,
mighty warriors were my steed
and Samalith allowed as
he had never seen such Love,
driven to find thee, dismounted
in stupor to grasp thy hand

Contrary nightful maintains
green ballast his coat
and ever searching
through algae-stained
murky pond moss
difficult to cross.
Replied he:
"Ever I the sword-bearer
lept the Hellespont of Love
to serve thy image."

"Where persimmons grow in plenty
and wrathful fields of poppies
climatus and cerwine weed
these green and glorious companions
were my preserves as I past
continents and sea waters on my left
and limped down the lifeline.

125

Of hopelessness filled with despair
at not finding thee."

"That apple of Joyfulness
I had left unmunched
when the controversy
among the Knight-field
sped into war
and blackness subsumed
the Camelot of our once mind
sweet dialogue that fruit
that savors Truth,
severed from the Vine."

"Now met, thou faithful White
like two pillage nerve channels
exhausted I nearly fall
as I reach for your clutch
having dreamed of none else
these erstwhile and suffering years
when the twain was split
I, Green Gawain
Comely in love of friend."

Searching, too, I, White
down the borders of Dwarfsville
where sputtering mouths mutter
the conflicting directions
and no one has seen the green
nor interpreted thy exploits
in the lexicon of gallantry,
I fast faced the North Wind
in the Siberian plain of bleating
friend loss

Gawain I loved thee
since those days in court
we both loved the same woman
and served the mighty Arthur
noble our lust for Truth
consummate in hope to
find the tinned and silver cup
touched by our Lord's own lips

Never out of mind
this ballasting, bare hope
in the divine and lustfree hope
to serve the King and God and Thee,
my friend whose blood
runs in veins prepared by
solitary nuns in Greece
a thousand years ago,
after our Lord's death.

"I service the high roads
and walk where prickle
may tear the flesh of my dear horse
limp among the brush
and brandish the sword
I, Green, dedicated to that Queen
who inspired our hope
in the everlasting crucible-bent cup."

"I sing of thee
when branches bent me in
and lumbered among the thicket
searching the way
thinking light and the next horizon
might bring me sight of thee
or some signpost
and inspiration of your whereabouts."

"Labor of love and of fasting
serveth the King and our Lord's holy blood
a day where flaxen-headed infidels
nodded in disbelief
I so clasped your image,
had walked so far empty on the shores
of that North Coast."

Should I put in words, actions
you require it not
should I notice syntax of love avowals
it is beneath my thought
I savored thy noble brow
I lasted the while of my pilgrimage
and now I live to embrace Thee
fellow knight, physician, Brother.

The Lama's Center in Me

When I think of my future
What I would like to be,
I remember a seated Lama
a hand on each knee,
I would like to be contained
in myself like he,
Three fish just breaking water
like before it seems to me
'Cept this time there's
a KNOWING self, to see.

I would be like the Lama
and contain in me the whole,
The cosmos of all wisdom
the majesty of soul,
I would walk in watch ways
where hurry takes no toll,
Oh, I would be the water
the crucible's own coal,
To be in Thy echo
is my solitude's goal.

Praise Thee natural,
form and also none,
I'd be in the rain's
gentle remembrance begun,
I'd be like Thy light
before end of day has spun,
The quiet of night earn
and with Thee in dreams, one.

The prattle of blowing fish
the light upon the path,
The wind that lies in wait
which then cometh and goeth,
The forlorn cry
and the inimitable laugh,
One fully realized being
such a laughter hath.

The God-image is not Dead

God is not dead.
Exit twenty centuries
and twenty-five in the East
Even more in Palestine
the tiers of Indians and Chinese,
Such an energy doesn't
roll over and die
e'en if mind would have it so,
Foundation of minds and being—
The god-image is not dead.

How do I know
I'm not counting on Aquinas
or Plotinus, Plato or Zeno,
The bridge to Newton's lab
is not so widely traveled,
Franklin had his fling
and while Jefferson's logic danced
I'm speaking beyond these,
in the direction of Walden Pond
and Spring's Great Thaw.

It's time for the great thaw
to come home to us
whether in tones of "emptiness,"
Buddha compassion or bliss,
sacred sense of history,
the still small voice,
Shiva dancing the world,
Mahabharata's echos,
depth analysis
Zen, or meditation.

Or the still small voice
poised by the Big Bang,

I know that to which
I belong is not dead
even as I live that
which gives form to formless ideas and
returns again to chaos
that number, that order
among disorder, is mine.

Praise the Jews and the Sufis
Praise animism
and shamanism, Christians,
tribesman, wonderful women,
mystics, Tibetan masters,
late and near wise
persons tuned to the spirit
of the universe, from everywhere,
they can't all be wrong;
more, the frequency alludes the receiver.

Some would rather anything
than anthropomorphism,
and anything we've got,
Hollywood and "image,"
culture's field is vacant
for a supreme idea;
then one not so supreme
moves in, takes over
the lonely house, the hovel,
bereft of any meaning.

There is someplace to look,
to the tenderness of a saint,
to the compassion of Ocean of Wisdom
to the song in the free mind
to the limits of reason,
assonance and synchronicity
subtleties of chaos theory,

one world underlying
matter and spirit,
inner world of Spirit.

If we humans are really
of the stuff of the whole
and awareness has come our way
then we could become
the universe's awareness,
look back on God,
be part of God,
as Meister Eckhart said;
God is not dead,
No division, Om.

They said God was dead
with Darwin's evolution,
if only the fittest survive
then no truck with morals;
yet newer science has proved
animal species depend
on each other, upon balance,
relativity's a more modern
seance, yet not so
powerful yet as hate.

That is our fate
to stop the bomb in anyone's
hands, the machine gun,
the psychopath's cry
of fire in the crowded theatre,
no matter the slogan;
without the god-image
how are you going to stop
these madmen
some claiming deity's will,

When no one's home at the top,
and the citadel vacant
which used to be reserved
for deity, then
the countryside is in turmoil,
technology doesn't change that,
When will we turn again
to find the god-image within,
Deity's more than
the secular state.

You would have to have
a completely different attitude,
Pindar's human virtues
crying out,
but for that you need
one inviolate,
incorruptible essence
born of the knowledge of good and evil
transcendent over personality
and born beyond time.

An essence beyond religion
and containing its essence,
a flow beyond words
and uttered,
a seeming passion
and letting go,
and experience beyond faith
and a faith in experience
a rootedness in life
and knowing the Beyond.

Where is the great thaw?
It is in the human heart
walking by nature's stream
shafts of greenest grass
emerging from warming ground,
the darkest death over

when no sound had been,
presence "walks" beside.
I talk to presence, "prayer"
in another land—before
biology, criticism,
self-conscious erudition—
at home where the soul
hears its own voice
shakes in delight with the new,
a winking star of the universe.

Notes

One - Inner Journey to Sacred Places

1. Walter Burkert, *Greek Religion*, Trans. Jim Raffan, Cambridge, Massachusetts, Harvard University Press, 1977, p. 269.
2. An inner woman dream figure mediates the psyche to a man's conscious life; anima is Latin for psyche (Greek) or soul. Jung says the anima shows the psyche or inner life, animated.
3. It is always advisable when one is opening up inner material, to have access to persons trained in this field.
4. Arnold Mindell, *Working with the Dreaming Body*, London, Routledge & Kegan Paul, 1985.
5. Vincent Scully, *The Earth, the Temple and the Gods*, New Haven, Yale University Press, 1979.
6. Ibid.
7. Ibid.
8. "In Touch," published by Centerpoint, Nashua, New Hampshire, Summer 1991, p. 2.
9. Scully, op.cit.
10. Mrs. Dora Kalff, Jungian analyst, pioneered work with children, and she utilized the mandala.
11. C. G. Jung, *Memories, Dreams, Reflections,* recorded and edited by Aniela Jaffe, translated by Richard and Clara Winston, New York, Vintage Books, 1965.
12. Ibid., p. 225.
13. Joseph Campbell, *The Power of Myth*, New York, Doubleday, 1988.
14. *The Horizon Book of Great Cathedrals*, editors of Horizon Magazine, introduction by Zoe Oldenbourg, New York, American Heritage Publishing Co., 1968, p. 257.

Two - Psychological Transformation Arising from the Transpersonal: The Experience of a Modern Nun

1. C. G. Jung, *The Archetypes of the Collective Unconscious*, collected works, Vol. 9, I. p. 324.
2. Larry E. Beutler et. al., "Inability to Express Intense Effect: A Common Link Between Depression and Pain," *The Journal of Consulting and Clinical Psychology,* Vol. 54, no. 6, December 1986, p. 757.

3."Four Filmed Interviews with Richard S. Evans," 1951, edited and rearranged version in *Conversations with Carl Jung*, Princeton, Van Nostrand, 1964.

4.C. G. Jung, "On the Psychology of the Unconscious," *Two Essays on Analytical Psychology*, collected works, Vol. 7, paragraph 194.

5.C. G. Jung, "On the Nature of Psyche," *On Psychic Energy*, collected works, Vol. 8, paragraph 418.

6."Approaching the Unconscious," *Man and His Symbols*, edited by, C. G. Jung, London, Aldus, 1964.

7.Arnold Mindell, *The Year I*, London, Arkana/Penguin, 1989, pp. 82-83.

8.*Julian Woman of Our Day*, edited by Robert Llewelyn, Mystic, Connecticut, Twenty-third Publications, 1987.

9.C. G. Jung, *Psychological Types*, collected works, Vol. 6, paragraph 717.

10.Matthew Fox, *Breakthrough: Meister Eckhart's Creation Spirituality in New Translation*, New York, Image Books, 1980, p. 2.

11.C. G. Jung, commentary to Richard Wilhelm's translation of *The Secret of the Golden Flower*, New York, Harcourt Brace Jovanovich, 1962, p. 93.

12.Psychological work with disease does not preclude work with physicians, and it is recommended that one try to utilize both.

13.C. G. Jung, *Aion: Researches into the Phenomenology of the Self*, collected works, Vol. 9, paragraph 170.

14.William H. Kennedy, "The American Unconscious," Centerpoint III, Nashua, New Hampshire, Centerpoint Foundation, sheet B, session 4, p. 4.

15.Miguel Serrano, *C. G. Jung and Hermann Hesse: A Record of Two Friendships*, translated by Frank MacShane, London, Routledge & Kegan Paul, 1977, pp. 85-86.

16.Tenzin Gyatso, *Freedom in Exile: The Autobiography of the Dalai Lama*, New York, A Cornelia & Michael Bessie Book, 1990, p. 270.

17.David Roomy, *Inner Work in the Wounded and Creative: The Dream in the Body*, London, Arkana/Penguin, 1990.

18. Modification of an idea of Arnold Mindell's.

Three - Centering & Healing . . . the Journey into the Mandala

1.Isaac Stern, *Carnegie Hall, One Hundred Year Anniversary Celebration*, Public Television, April 1991.

2.Barbara Hannah, *Encounters with the Soul: Active Imagination as Developed by C.G. Jung*, Santa Monica, California, Sigo Press, 1981.

3.Amy Mindell, "The Hidden Dance: An Introduction to Process—oriented Movement Work," Master's Thesis, Antioch University, Yellow Springs, Ohio, 1986.

4.Arnold Mindell, *Working on Yourself Alone: Inner Dreambody Work*, London, Arkana/Penguin, 1990.

5.C. G. Jung, *The Symbolic Life*, collected works, Vol. 18, paragraph 799.

6.David Roomy, *Inner Work in the Wounded and Creative: The Dream in the Body*, London and New York, Arkana/Penguin, 1990.

7.C. G. Jung, *Psychology and Alchemy*, collected works, Vol. 12.

8.C. G. Jung, *Psychology and Alchemy*, collected works, Vol. 12, pp. 28-29.

Four - The Diamond Body & the Centering Process

1.Marie-Louise von Franz, *On Dreams and Death*, translated by Emmanuael Xipolitas Kennedy and Vernon Brooks, Boston and London, Shambala, 1987.

2.C. G. Jung, *Memories, Dreams, Reflections*, edited by Aniela Jaffe, translated by Richard and Clara Winston, New York, Vintage Books, 1965, pp. 197-199.

3.*The Secret of the Golden Flower*, translated by Richard Wilhelm, foreword and commentary by C. G. Jung,, London, Routledge and Kegan Paul, 1965, fig. 10, p. 136 ff. The yellow castle painting can also be found in C. G. Jung, *The Archetypes of the Collective Unconscious*, collected works, Vol. 9, fig. 36, p. 356 ff.

4.C. G. Jung, *Word and Image*, edited by Aniela Jaffe, Princeton, Princeton University Press, 1979, p. 93.

5.It is important to emphasize here that I do not mean the city in its outer sense. That city, as we know, is often today the focus of some of the most destructive forces of modern life. I shall return to this problem at a later point.

6.C. G. Jung, *Psychology and Alchemy*, collected works,Vol. 12, pp. 79 and 124.

7.Ibid., p. 265.

8.Venhata Ramanan, *Nagarjuna's Philosophy*, Delhi Motilal Banarsidass, 1987, p. 226.

9.D.T. Suzuki, *Mysticism: Christian and Buddhist, the Eastern and Western Way*, New York, The MacMillan Company, 1957, p. 50., quoting translation of Eckhart by Raymond B. Blakney, Harper and Brothers, New York, 1941, p. 231.

10.Miguel Serrano, *C. G. Jung and Hermann Hesse: A Record of Two Friendships*, translated by Frank MacShane, London, Routledge and Kegan Paul, 1966.

11.C. G. Jung, *Dream Analysis: Notes of the Seminar Given in 1928-30*, edited by William McGuire, Princeton, Princeton University Press, 1984.

Five - The Ancient City as Symbol of the Individuation Process

1.C. G. Jung, *Psychology and Alchemy*, collected works, Vol. 12, p. 41.

2.C. G. Jung, *The Practice of Psychology*, collected works, Vol. 16, p. 311.

3.*Psychology and Alchemy*, p. 53.

4.Ibid., p. 82.

5.Ibid.

6.Ibid., p. 11.

7.Ibid., p. 86.
8.Ibid., p. 41.
9.Ibid., p. 103.
10.Ibid., p. 306.
11.Ibid., p. 114.
12.Ibid., p. 124.
13.Ibid., p. 118.
14.Ibid.
15.Ibid., pp. 114-115.
16.Ibid., p. 120.
17.Ibid, p. 114.
18.Ibid., pp. 129-131.
19.Arnold Mindell, *Dreambody: The Body's Role in Revealing the Self,* Santa Monica, Sigo Press, 1982, p. 113.
20.Arnold Mindell, *Working with the Dreaming Body*, London, Routledge and Kegan Paul, 1985, p. 45.
21.Ibid., p. 124.
22.Ibid.
23.M. R. James, translator, *The Apocryphal New Testament*, Oxford, 1924, pp. 27 ff (as quoted by Jung).

Six - The Ancient City—Amplification of its Historical & Archeological Meanings

1.Lewis Mumford, *The City in History: Its Origins, Its Transformations, and Its Prospects*, New York and London, Harcourt Brace Jovanovich, Publishers, 1961, p. 95.
2.Ibid., p. 102.
3.Ibid., p. 110.
4.Ibid.
5.Ibid., p. 97.
6.Ibid., p. 98.
7.C. G. Jung, *Psychology and Alchemy*, collected works, Vol. 12, p. 53.
8.Miguel Serrano, *C. G. Jung and Hermann Hesse: A Record of Two Friendships*, translated by Frank MacShane, London, Routledge and Kegan Paul, 1966.
9.Arnold Mindell, *City Shadows: Psychological Interventions in Psychiatry,* London, Routledge and Kegan Paul, 1988.
10.Karen Gram, "The Vancouver Sun," March 16, 1992.
11.Arnold Mindell, *The Year I,* Global Process Work, London, Arkana, 1989.

Seven - The Importance of Dreams, Myths, & Mercurius

1.Akira Kurosawa, *Dreams*, Japan.

2.Joseph Campbell, *Hero with a Thousand Faces*, Princeton, Princeton University Press, 1973.

3.Arnold Mindell, *River's Way: The Process Science of the Dreambody*, London, Routledge & Kegan Paul, 1985.

4.Marie-Louise von Franz, *An Introduction to the Interpretation of Fairy Tales*, Dallas, Spring Publications, 1982, p.17.

5.Arnold Mindell, *The Year I.*

6.C. G. Jung, "The Spirit Mercurius," *Alchemical Studies*, collected works, Vol. 13, Princeton, Princeton University Press, 1976.

7.Karl Kerenyi, *Hermes Guide of Souls: The Mythologem of the Masculine Source of Life*, translated by Murray Stein, Dallas, Spring Publications, Inc., 1986, p. 3.

8.Ibid., Marie-Louise von Franz.

9.C. G. Jung, "Answer to Job," *Psychology and Religion*, collected works, Vol. 11, pp. 335-474.

10.William Kennedy was a lifelong friend of Jung and during the sixties was the president of the C. G. Jung Foundation of New York. He was the executive director, and I, the associate director of the Episcopal Council for Foreign Students, which brought psychological awareness into an important cross-cultural program .

11.Arnold Mindell, *The Year I.*

12.Chretien de Troyes, *Perceval or The Story of the Grail*, translated by Ruth Harwood Cline, Athens, The University of Georgia Press, 1983, p. 173.

13.*Teachings of Rumi, the Masnavi*, translated by E. H. Whinfield, New York, E. P. Hutton & Co., Inc., 1975, p. 171.

Eight - Intuitions of Connections to Other Times as a Modern Process

1.C. G. Jung, *Archetypes of the Collective Unconscious*, collected works, Vol. 9, p. 28.

2.C. G. Jung, *Memories, Dreams, Reflections*, edited by Aniela Jaffe, New York, Vintage, 1965, p. 286.

3.Ibid., p. 287.

4.Robin Lane Fox, *Pagans and Christians*, San Francisco, Harper & Row, 1986.

5.An idea from Jung.

6.*Oriental Splendor*, edited by Herbert van Thal, London, New English Library, Ltd., 1962, p. 40.

7.C. G. Jung, et al., *Man and His Symbols*, London, Aldus, 1964.

8. Ibid., p. 196.

9.Rosemary Gordon, *Dying and Creating, A Search for Meaning*, London, The Society of Analytical Psychology, 1978.

10.Arnold Mindell, *The Dreambody in Relationships*, London and New York, Arkana, 1988.

11.Arnold Mindell, *The Year I and The Header as Martial Artist: An Introduction to Deep Democracy*, Harper Collins, San Francisco, 1992.

Epilogue: The Grail and a Modern Dreamer's Quest

1.Ean and Dieke Begg, *In Search of the Holy Grail and the Precious Blood*, London, Thorsons, 1995.
2.Emma Jung and Marie-Louise von Franz, translated by Andrea Dykes, *The Grail Legend*, Boston, Sigo Press, 1986, p. 122.
3.Ibid., p. 18.
4.Ibid., Emma Jung quoting in part an alchemical text, pp.142-143.
5.Ibid., p. 109.
6.Ibid., p. 300.